Nurtured Heart Play – Integrating the Nurtured Heart Approach® into Facilitated Game Play: A Guide for Educators, Out-of-School Program Providers, Therapists, and Parents

For information contact:

Nurtured Heart Publications
4165 West Ironwood Hill Drive
Tucson, Arizona 85745
E-mail: adhddoc@theriver.com

For information about bulk purchasing discounts of this book or other Nurtured Heart Approach books, CDs or DVDs and for orders within the book industry, please contact Brigham Distributing at 435-723-6611.

Cover Art by Alice Glasser
Cover Design and Book Design by Owen DeLeon - Owen Visual Communication
Editing by Melissa Lynn Lowenstein
Prolong Press Limited –Hong Kong
Library of Congress Card Catalogue Number: Pending
ISBN 978-0-9826714-9-8

Printed in China
First Printing: December 2017

NURTURED HEART

PLAY

*Integrating the Nurtured Heart Approach®
into Facilitated Game Play:
A Guide for Educators, Out-of-School Program
Providers, Therapists, and Parents*

HOWARD MOODY

WITH HOWARD GLASSER, ALICE GLASSER
AND MELISSA LOWENSTEIN

TABLE OF CONTENTS

WHY NURTURED HEART PLAY?

It is a happy talent to know how to play.

— Ralph Waldo Emerson

I was meeting a seven-year-old boy for his first play therapy session. He was adopted at birth by a wonderful, loving family with high expectations of their only son. The week before, in a meeting with me, the parents described a little boy who was very dysregulated, prone to big tantrums, oppositional, and very smart. They told me that he had problems at school with rushing through his work, getting off-task, and acting out at times.

In the session, I used a game called Kerplunk to help him identify his feelings and build a therapeutic relationship. In setting up the game, you pick up sticks through a small hole on one side of a cylinder and then through a hole on the other side. It can be frustrating and a little difficult at times. I used this opportunity to energize the good choices the little guy was making in handling his frustration. I said several times, "Look at you! Although it is hard to find the hole, you don't give up. I can see that you are very patient."

He gave me a skeptical look each time, and would then continue to play. When I saw him start to get frustrated but continue trying, I praised his patience and persistence. About the third time I did this, he stopped me and said, "I'm not patient."

"Why do you think that?" I asked. He shared that his parents had

told him he was not patient. I said, "Well they must have not seen you do this, because I've seen you be very patient at least three times in the last 10 minutes. So now, you are patient!"

The little boy looked up at his mother who was sitting on the couch observing the session and said, "Did you hear that, Mom? I think I just learned to be patient!" His mother was then also able to acknowledge his newfound skill. This little boy is a great example of someone seeing himself in a new light! Powerful stuff!

— *Play therapist and Nurtured Heart Approach trainer* Lyla Tyler

I've been a play specialist since 1978. I know that intentional use of games and other playful activities provides a joyful and effective space for growth, connection, and learning. In 2012, I discovered Howard Glasser's Nurtured Heart Approach, a proven method for bringing out the best in kids. I quickly saw the potential of combining it with the PlayShops I've brought to thousands of children and adults over the last several decades. That synthesis yielded Nurtured Heart Play, which is the topic of this book.

Children's primary mode of being is play. It is how they experience, discover, and engage with the world around them. And play is important for everyone – especially play that is open-hearted and connected, where we feel alive and present. Weaving the Nurtured Heart Approach into play, we build young people's inner wealth by giving them direct experiences of success and calling out their greatness. The essence of play is connection, and the Nurtured Heart Approach is about connecting in deeply, expansively positive ways that nourish everyone involved.

If you are already familiar with NHA, this book provides a ready-made collection of activities, resources, and concepts about play that will enhance your application and appreciation of this breakthrough modality. If you are new to NHA, this book can be a companion volume as you master the basics. Intentional, guided

Nurtured Heart Play provides a fun 'laboratory' in which to develop and hone your mastery of the Approach.

The Nurtured Heart Approach is all about intentionally energizing the positive aspects of behavior, being very clear with behavior boundaries and rules, and purposefully recognizing and appreciating the special qualities in everyone. Play is all about possibilities, imagination, creativity, and fun. Bringing these two powerful elements together is truly a win-win situation.

While the NHA process can be brought into all kinds of childhood play – tag games, board games, sports activities, dance, art, playing pretend – the games in this book have been specifically selected to create an environment conducive to positive experiences for everyone. And, as it turns out, these principles can help to create a state of being that is not only good for the body, mind, and spirit, but is also a lot of fun. The games featured in this collection are especially well designed for practicing the techniques of expressing appreciation, recognizing each other's greatness, and having clear guidelines that allow for playful energy to emerge and flow.

Nurtured Heart Play reminds us to take time to note the wonderful qualities being exhibited by everyone playing; to step out of the absorption and flow of the game to acknowledge players for the greatness they are living while immersed in play; and to be clear with rules and boundaries so everyone can feel safe and included while having an experience of having the power and wisdom to actively participate. It gives us a language of appreciation with which to energize everyone involved. It holds us in the present moment: in our joy, in our creativity and imagination, saying yes to life, saying yes to each other, energizing each other's greatness.

CHAPTER ONE

AN
INTRODUCTION
TO NURTURED HEART PLAY

In the early formative years, play is almost synonymous
with life. It is second only to being nourished, protected
and loved. It is the basic ingredient of physical, intellectual,
social and emotional growth.

— Ashley Montague, *The Play Specialist*

Play is vital to all humanity. It is the finest
system of education known to man.

— Neville Scarge

Play is the natural expression of kids when they are happy. It's
like breathing to them, primary and necessary. Yet, do we adults
understand it anymore? Do we truly appreciate the importance and
the magic of play? Do we give it the attention it deserves?

Maybe not. We aren't doing a very good job of creating adequate
space and time for kids to play. Kids have less and less access to
the natural world, less freedom to explore their neighborhoods and
create their own cooperative games, and less play time at school
than they need. Academics tend to be considered unserious, frivo-
lous, or even useless when they incorporate elements of play. The
arts – incredibly rich arenas for inspired play – are disappearing
from public schools as budget crunches dictate. As adults, most of
us have given up on any authentic form of play in our own lives.
We're too busy to waste time just playing, right? It's all we can do

to just find the time to work out, or maybe watch some sports or our favorite shows on TV. Maybe some of us play a structured game here and there, or a smartphone game. But full-out, physical, interactive play? Not for grown-ups. Right?

Wrong. Neuroscientists, developmental biologists, psychologists, and researchers from every point of the scientific compass have come to recognize that play is a crucial biological process – not only for children, but for human beings of all ages. It has evolved over eons in animal species; and, like any behavior that makes it through the ongoing process of natural selection, it has survival value. Play shapes the brain and makes animals smarter and more adaptable. In higher animals, it fosters empathy and is pivotal in allowing complex social groups to form. For humans, play lies at the core of creativity, innovation, and socialization. Existentially, play is an expression of our humanity and our individuality. Play is the way we learn to cooperate and co-create. It is an important part of who we are, and a place we feel most alive.

Even as it's squeezed out of our schools and (increasingly) homes in a time where many preschoolers are over-structured, overscheduled, or watching screens instead of playing, more and more educators and scholars are seeing a clear need to treat play as the spectacularly rich source of learning, growth and connection that it is. However you have come to this volume, I imagine you are part of that growing quorum of people who are tired of being told that you should dismiss an experience as educational or valuable just because it's fun. I want to personally thank you for being here! Let's breathe a mutual sigh of relief...and dive in.

My hope for this book is that it will support you in creating healthy, dynamic, positive guided play experiences that help children feel safe, enriched and connected. Within this context, opportunities to blend in the Nurtured Heart Approach are endless. This chapter will provide a brief, play-centric overview and introduction to the NHA, which will be fleshed out further in descriptions of the games in the latter part of the book. If you have not had a more general introduction to the approach yet, I recommend you read one of Howard Glasser's books on the Nurtured Heart Approach. Those books are listed in the Resources section at the end of this book.

Begin by Honoring the Child in Yourself

Your own spirit of play is what will bring out the best in participants in all of the activities described in this book. One recent participant said to me after a PlayShop, "We are all really just kids in grown-up bodies." In all of us, there is still a childlike part that needs to be seen and heard; that wants to be accepted and acknowledged; that wants to play. The Nurtured Heart Approach works best when adopted in a spirit of play, curiosity, and creativity.

So, although this book is meant to be a toolkit for working with children, remember that it is also meant to spark that part of you that wants to play, laugh, and celebrate life. Connecting to that joyful, childlike part of you will help you be a more effective, supportive, and caring teacher, facilitator, parent, counselor, and role model/inspiration for all the children in your life.

A Brief Introduction to the Nurtured Heart Approach®

The Nurtured Heart Approach is designed to help us discover, uncover, and express our greatness. Anyone trained in the Nurtured Heart Approach has learned how to lead people into this discovery. Here, I'll give a brief introduction – hopefully, enough to help you use Nurtured Heart Play in your home, classroom or program. The terminology and techniques in this section will be brought back when specific games are discussed; refer back to this section or the wrap-up at the end of this chapter as needed as you begin to work with the games themselves.

An important component of the NHA and of Nurtured Heart

Play is the spirit within which you are leading and setting the tone for the process, honoring uniqueness, and appreciating your fellow players. It's more than positivity; it's more like a soul-level drive to help children remember who they really are as great young people. The Nurtured Heart Approach points out that it's a tendency in our DNA to see what is wrong with the picture, which leads to our giving problems most of our attention. Most of us have a built-in ease when it comes to spouting language about what is negative. This negativity bias is deeply encoded in our biological systems; our brains are geared towards avoiding danger. We wouldn't be here unless our ancestors were sufficiently talented at seeing and acting upon what's wrong with the picture. And the modern-day version is that we are often equally talented at spotting when things aren't going right—and with waxing poetic about every nuance of problems.

Ongoing work in neuroscience has led to an understanding that our brains are hard-wired for negativity. The ability to see even small increments of what's wrong is part of the instinctive programming that has enabled humanity to make it this far. Seeing our everyday lives through this negative lens, however, leads us to focus on our worries, miseries, and doubts (what Glasser calls WMDs). To shift negative bias to positive, we have to consciously work on inputting positivity. Compelling science in the field of positive psychology supports how helpful it is to input positive expressions into our lives. Gratitude, appreciation, acknowledgment, and recognition are powerful ways to create optimism, heart centeredness, and even good health. Brain science increasingly reinforces that actively focusing on positives can actually change the hardwiring of our brains in ways that make positivity more natural with practice.

Howard Glasser developed this approach to support parents in guiding their difficult children to use their intensity differently. As a child and family therapist, Glasser found that the traditional methods he was using to try to help families with intense children were not only ineffective – they were backfiring. He began to tune in to the energetics of the interactions between these parents and children, and to re-experience the way the dynamics worked in his own history as a challenging child. He arrived at a series of insights that helped him to shift the way he was working with children and families, and was able to encapsulate them in a few stories and principles. The approach that evolved from that point turned out to have a dramatically positive impact not only on difficult children, but on all children – and on the adults who were learning and applying the approach as well.

Here are some of the stories and principles that "downloaded" for Glasser as he evolved the Nurtured Heart Approach. The throughline is to become aware of the ways in which adults inadvertently "energize" behaviors they don't want and fail to do so with the behaviors they DO want, and how we might take steps to flip this dynamic:

- **You as a child's favorite toy:** When a child gets a new toy, he doesn't read the instructions; he just starts to play. He experiments to see what creates the most interesting responses to his manipulations. He drinks in impressions based on the response of the toy. If a feature yields a no response or a low-energy response, he tends to move on. This Nurtured Heart notion holds that, to children, the adults who care for them are essentially the most amazing, fascinating toys in the world. The child constantly drinks in energetic impressions of what will get the toys to respond; from the very earliest months of that child's life, she is developing a concept of which "buttons" yield interesting and compelling responses and which yield little or nothing intriguing. Adults tend to react much more strongly and quickly when things are going wrong: when rules are broken or when a child is acting out or threatening to act out. When things are going well, adults tend to connect with less excitement and engagement. Glasser will often use the example of a parent seeing two children playing together nicely, and purposely not saying anything for fear of disrupting the moment and triggering something more negative! We adults tend to let a lot of children's good choices go by unacknowledged. Kids learn early on that a reliable way to get their "favorite toy" to respond is to rule-break or push boundaries. No matter how busy we might be, it's rare that we are too busy to dive into a problem. We have a notion that a problem means we really need to show up in energized ways.

- **A difficult child is actually an intense child:** Glasser chooses to re-frame "difficult" or "challenging" as "intense." The intense child requires more: more connection, more stimulation, stronger limits. She has more life force and has a harder time managing and directing it. When that same child has formed the impression that the way to get more is to act out, that is what she'll do, reliably – and standard disciplinary methods to get her to stop tend only to throw gasoline on the fire of misbehavior, which they do by trying to teach lessons in the midst of the problem: more energy to negativity.

Entering into the land of play gives us a golden opportunity to model self-regulation and interpersonal sensitivity in action for children at all levels of intensity. Playing with kids is a way to meet exuberance across the full spectrum of its expression, and to give it beautiful direction.

Children instinctively want to play, and virtually every child is willing to act within the boundaries required by the game – often, for long spans of attention. For children who carry a lot of intensity, however, angling for negative attention can trump this natural desire to participate in non-disruptive ways. The Nurtured Heart Approach offers a reliable way to work with the energy of intensity rather than squashing it or making it wrong.

Intense children are more likely to experience a buildup of pressure – like steam in their biological systems. When that energy is suppressed, it can get to a point where it is released in the form of those behaviors we find most difficult. NHA Play releases those energies in a healthy way while positively meeting the intense child's need for deep connection. Many of these games can be plugged in between learning sessions for a few minutes at a time, giving the kids a moment of fun and a chance to release suppressed energy in constructive ways.

Video games and technology are taking up increasing amounts of children's time – time they might otherwise spend moving or interacting playfully, preferably outdoors. Children need to move their bodies, to be out in nature, and express themselves fully during play. With the question of safety in neighborhoods and with an emphasis on early academics in schools, kids are simply not getting the play, engagement, or connection they need. Since play is a dynamic way in which to provide interaction, and since the Nurtured Heart Approach is a highly effective method for connecting in positive ways with children, blending the two together is truly a win-win.

I have two sons, Braden and Gavin, who are six and eight. My youngest is beautifully intense. They love to accompany me when I do graduate presentations about the Nurtured Heart Approach. Sometimes I integrate them into my talks, particularly when I am discussing intensity. I tell the class that although intensity is something that many people fear, it's just about learning to dance with it; it is not your enemy. And I say to my youngest son, "Would you call yourself intense?" And his response is always, "Yes." How wonderful that he is so aware of who he is, and he is not afraid of that. And when you drop that fear of who you are, and own it, it's really life-changing.

One day Braden came home from school and said, "Mommy, I have a really good story for you. I was in class and having a hard time keeping my hands to myself. I was about to tickle and push my friend, and then, Mommy, I stopped myself."

"Well, Braden," I said, "what was that an example of?"

"That was self-control, wasn't it, Mommy?"

"Absolutely, that's self-control."

Then my older son was so nurturing. He said, "Wow, Braden, I am really proud of you. That really takes a lot of effort."

And that's the way my boys talk to each other. I so love that they have the language to express that.

- Vivian Barajas, *NHA trainer and parent*

These two concepts – the "favorite toy" and intensity – help to explain how adults almost universally give more of their energy and attention to children when things are going wrong, and how some children respond to this by misbehaving in order to get MORE from the adults in their lives. Glasser describes this as "upside-down energy" – like telling a child not to misbehave, and then giving the child $100 every time he does!

The Nurtured Heart Approach upholds that in order to change a challenging child's behavior, this energy needs to be re-aligned to be right-side up. Adults need to withhold as much of their energy, vitality and relationship as possible when negativity is happening (while giving a true consequence that is 'un-energized' if a rule is broken), and then to pour it on when the child isn't doing the problem behavior. This is a practice designed to illuminate the child's inherent greatness and to build what Glasser calls Inner Wealth™ – a deep belief in one's self and in one's own greatness.

Turning this energy around requires adhering to The 3 Stands™ of the Nurtured Heart Approach.

The 3 Stands ——

1. **Absolutely No!** I refuse to energize negativity.

This means we don't give negative choices or rule-breaking any more energy than necessary to maintain safety. We do not lecture, warn, reprimand or scold. This Stand provides the foundation for the other two. If we do not remove the energetic charge and connectivity around negativity, the child won't respond nearly as well to the other two Stands or to the techniques of the Approach. It usually requires some internal work on cultivating the ability to "reset" yourself when you are tempted to reactively give your energy to negativity.

Does this mean we ignore problem behaviors? No! We enforce rules at all times using a specific consequence, which I'll describe shortly. But this first Stand demands that you resolve not to give yourself – the gift of you, of your energy and re-lationship – to what you don't want. As Glasser likes to say, "Why water weeds?"

Applying the First Stand to NHA Play

The beauty of play is that, in general, children want the connection and engagement that comes during play. If you have explained what the rules of the game are, and the expected kinds of actions, the boundaries of behavior should be clear. Anything outside those bounds is simply given a quick reset. The point is to not get caught up in the undesired behavior in any way whatsoever. Don't spend any time on what is off the topic of what is going well.

If the child isn't breaking a rule about behavior or game play but is going in that direction, you can apply this stand the way family therapist Valerie Potts does in her practice with families. Watch as the child starts to see where the real rewards are – in *following* the rules – and shifts in that direction.

> When I am playing with families, everyone is laughing and focusing on the game. When someone gets distracted or frustrated, even in a small way, it's my chance to model the Stand of "Absolutely No." I model this Stand indirectly by bringing attention to what they are doing that is right rather than what they are doing that isn't – such as telling a story about their day in the middle of the game – to getting frustrated with their younger sister because she is not holding their hand right. My focus stays on the game and what is happening that is supposed to be happening for us all to enjoy playing together. This includes when a child or a parent does something to get back to being pur-

poseful: for example, the child stops talking about their day or stops wiggling their hand, or tells their sibling to stop without yelling or jerking away or stomping off. Other things I notice are rules being followed, making eye contact with others in the game, holding their position in Human Statue, or taking their turn even though they don't want to be here because their day was exhausting and difficult.

— Valerie Potts, *NHA therapist and trainer*

2. **Absolutely Yes!** I resolve to relentlessly energize the positive – including anything that is not going wrong. I resolve to reflect the child's greatness in order to build his/her Inner Wealth.

This Stand sets an intention to acknowledge *non-negative* choices out loud, using positive insights to connect with the child. It replaces connection in negativity with connection around every level of progressing or constructive choice-making by the child – including any choice to *not* break a rule.

Tolltaker, Miracles from Molecules and Baby Steps refer to helpful and inspiring intentions that build a foundation for seeing and remarking upon positive choices many times each day, and four NHA techniques give more concrete guidance about how to find and comment on those positive choices.

- **Baby Steps:** Imagine yourself watching a baby take its first steps. Feel the wonder and thrill. Feel your heart spring open. You wouldn't dream of criticizing or correcting a baby's first steps; rather, you would only find ways to be excited and appreciative. This is the spirit in which the NHA asks you to see every step your child takes toward success. Don't take anything for granted.

- **The Tolltaker:** The story is that a college professor was driving across the San Francisco Bay Bridge and saw a tolltaker dancing happily in his booth. He was able to maneuver over there, and asked the tolltaker why he was so happy. "Are you kidding?" the tolltaker answered. "I have the best job in the world. I get to meet nice people all day and I have an incredible view! Besides, I'm studying to be a dancer, so if I dance while I'm here, I'm basically getting paid to practice. I'm out in the fresh air, getting exercise." The professor said, "Why aren't the other toll takers seeing things your way?" and the tolltaker answered, "Oh, those guys in the stand-up coffins? They're no fun!" Same job, same set of circumstances, completely different attitude: this tolltaker knew he could choose to be grateful and happy about certain aspects of his job, and to not give energy to complaints about exhaust fumes, unpleasant customers, or having to be on his feet. He chose to celebrate what he liked about being there. We always get to choose how we see things; is the cup half full, or half empty? In fact, *we are never not choosing.* We may as well choose to see things in a positive light. It can even be on a level beyond seeing the cup half-full or half-empty. We can choose whatever we can imagine, even if the cup is empty all the way!

- **Miracles from Molecules:** Fundamentally, this is the opposite of making mountains out of molehills. It's taking the whole skillset of focusing in on details of negativity and, instead of making a big deal over slivers of failure or misbehavior, practicing taking even a small success or the *absence* of misbehavior and building it up into an expansive reflection of the child's greatness.

This concept asks us to "break it down and add it up" – to acknowledge even the child's modest moves in the direction of successes, or steps toward desirable outcomes (the child gets up on time in the morning despite wanting to sleep in; brushes her teeth; puts on her seatbelt; eats her breakfast; does not fight with a sibling). In a games context, you could acknowledge the child standing up to participate; being enthusiastic without being disruptive; having dressed properly to play; or standing near a friend without talking out of turn. For a child who is painfully shy or often sits out, you can energize the child's just staying in the room. Acknowledge how hard this can be, reflecting the many contributing choices that support the child's wisdom and courage. The possibilities are limitless. These three intentions can all strongly contribute to the purposeful creation of successes for the children in our care. We are limited only by our imaginations in how far we can take them. They intentionally propel the techniques of the approach that follow.

The Nurtured Heart Techniques for Upholding the Second Stand

This approach is about more than "catching kids being good." It is about developing skills to see and acknowledge what is going right in vivid detail; about the art of creating goodness through our choices; and about leading the child to see more of who he or she really is, as a fine person: "This is where and how your greatness is showing up...RIGHT NOW."

For most, the idea of coming up with an ongoing stream of positive acknowledgements is intimidating, especially when a child tends to be difficult or challenging. Here are the techniques Glasser developed to build capacity for seeing and eloquently describing children's positive choices. Work with one technique at a time, building from the first to the last as you feel mastery happening. Eventually, they all will naturally flow together. Practice giving at least 10 recognitions per day to start. Typically, this will add up to just a few impactful minutes of intervention per day. Each appreciation takes only a few seconds.

Active Recognition: Report what you observe as though describing it to a blind person or to someone who isn't in the room; no judgment, good or bad. Active recognition works especially well with children who are highly resistant. Simply through the statement of inarguable truths, this form of recognition helps begin to convert upside-down energy by making the child feel seen, acknowledged and appreciated when not doing anything wrong. These comments lend themselves to children forming a new impression: that they need not act out to have relationship. They are seen, meaningful and valued for so much more than that.

"Jimmy, I want to acknowledge you for holding onto your friend's hands until the game was finished."

"Cami, when your friend next to you bent down to go through the hula hoop, you bent down too."

"David, you kept your body from running into anyone else as you crossed the circle."

"Jackson, you were smiling and laughing throughout the entire game!"

Notice that these acknowledgments have no value judgment. They simply express the adult's emotional engagement and a deep noticing of the child when things are going well. There is no commentary on how well they play; they get that simply by getting in the game, they are worth noticing.

Experiential Recognition: Add an acknowledgement of positive values or qualities of greatness.

"Kim, you are standing there so still while the rest of the group gets into position. You have incredible discipline and self-control right now."

"Jamie, I saw you raise your arm when it was Lisa's turn to go through the hula hoop. That took focus, collaboration and helpfulness."

"David, when you didn't get a seat and it was your turn to go into the middle, you did it without fussing. You allowed yourself to be vulnerable, which took courage and determination on your part. Both are great qualities."

"Ben, I noticed that you stayed right with the flow of the exercise. You were paying excellent attention and being wonderfully present."

Qualities of Greatness/Values to Acknowledge During Nurtured Heart Play

A good friend

A great listener

A helper

Able

Appreciative

Attentive

Authentic

Aware

Balanced

Being powerful

Being wise

Brave

Brilliant

Centered

Clear

Collaborative

Committed

Compassionate

Competent

Connected to others

Conscientious

Considerate

Content

Cooperative

Courageous

Courteous

Creative

Curious

Dedicated

Deliberate

Delightful

Determined

Diligent

Direct

Disciplined

Dynamic

Empathetic

Energetic

Enthusiastic

Even-tempered

Exceeding expectations

Excited

Expressive

Exuberant

Fair

Faithful

Fast

Fearless

Flexible

Focused

Forgiving

Funny

Generous

Gentle

Genuine

Giving

Glorious

Good hearted

Graceful

Gracious

Hardworking
Having an open mind
Helpful
Honest
Honorable
Humble
Humorous
Independent
Inquisitive
Inspiring
Intelligent
Intuitive
Joyous
Judicious
Kind
Kindhearted
Lighthearted
Likeable
Logical
Looking out for others
Loving
Making good choices
Managing your time well
Mindful
Modest
Motivated
Neat
Nice
Observant

Open minded
Organized
Passionate
Patient
Peaceful
Persistent
Pleasant
Polite
Positive
Powerful
Purposeful
Questioning
Quiet
Reasonable
Receptive to new ideas
Relentless
Reliable
Respectful
Respecting self
Seeing the big picture
Self-controlled
Showing integrity
Sincere
Steadfast
Strong on the inside
Tactful
Teachable
Tenacious
Tenderhearted
Thankful

Trustworthy
Understanding
Uplifting
Vibrant
Vigilant
Visionary
Warm
Welcoming
Wise
Zestful

Once values are incorporated into recognitions, freely begin to call out the child's greatness. Think in terms of all the positive choices emanating from a core of greatness that has been in that child since the day he or she was born. Credit that natural greatness, and the child who is expressing it, with all the positive choices you can. For example, "You're brave" can become "You have the greatness of bravery," and can then be followed with a few words giving incontrovertible evidence that this is true.

Proactive Recognition: Acknowledgement of rules NOT broken. This gives you vast territory for positive acknowledgement, especially when rules are stated in a "No..." format: "No hitting. No leaving your bed unmade. No fighting with your sister." Glasser recommends re-casting so-called "positive rules" like "Be kind" and "Be respectful" as a list of rules that begin with "No." The line between rule followed and rule broken is far clearer this way, and gives much more room for positive statements. In this context, the more rules you have, the better, because there is more positive acknowledgement available around every rule when it is not being broken.

Since a certain amount of play is rule-based, particularly as kids get older, you have a unique opportunity to focus in on this type of recognition during play. You'll see examples of ways to use this type of recognition as you move into the part of this book where games are described.

"Lisa, I noticed how you started to move around towards the end of the human knot game, but you didn't let go of the hands you were holding; neither did you let yourself get frustrated with those around you. You stayed in the game until we finished and didn't let your need

to move keep you from following the rules of the game. You stuck with it, and that takes self-control and determination."

"David, not once were you distracting to the others while I was explaining the game, and that takes maturity and good judgment."

"Latisha, you joined with Kim very smoothly, without hitting or falling into her. You followed the rules of the game beautifully, and that took perseverance!"

"Ben, I see you standing there smiling, and holding the other kids' hands without jerking or twirling around. You are focused and determined to have fun with your friends. I see the greatness of your joy."

"Mary Lee, have you ever thrown a fit when someone says no to you? Do you have that power? Now, you're using your power and wisdom to NOT do that. I bet it feels good to be so in charge!"

You can always incorporate greatness recognition as an addition: *"You have the greatness of self-control, power and wisdom!"*

The Barometer of Not-Great

Think of anything that could be happening now that would be not great. How not great would it be if a student were arguing and swearing right now, or if a child was refusing to participate? How not great would it be if five students were breaking rules at once instead of just one? Right – it could potentially be very not-great. Therefore, how great is it that these and other challenging issues are not coming up right now?

This playful and somewhat strange line of thinking has been an amazing barometer for dialing into degrees of gratitude of which we might not otherwise be aware. Practice expressing this level of appreciation with others in a play situation or in everyday life. This is Proactive Recognition in action.

Creative Recognition: Where an adult "hijacks" a child into a successful moment by ensuring compliance with a request, giving 100% of the credit to that person for doing something good/right/ great. Normal requests that begin with "Please... Can you...Would you...?" imply a choice; it's best to jump to clearer forms of request such as, "Here's what I need." Taking this even further, we can insert a child directly into requests that are already in the process of being fulfilled or have already been fulfilled.

(Noah comes into the room and puts his backpack in the proper place.) *"Noah, come on in and put your backpack where it belongs... Wow, you did that so quickly. I appreciate your respect for the group – you're doing all you need to do to support all of us in getting started on time."*

(Katie approaches Jimmy in a game where they are meant to partner up.) *"Katie, please partner up with Jimmy."* (She does.) *"Thanks for immediately coming over and not arguing about being Jimmy's partner. You showed responsibility and respect for me and everyone else playing the game...and Jimmy, you stopped talking immediately when I made that request and did exactly what I asked. Awesome!"*

(Ben and David run towards the hula-hoops scattered across the lawn; teacher heads in their direction.) *"Hey, Ben and David, I was just going to ask you both to go around and pick up the hula hoops, but I see that you are already doing it! Wow, you are both on it today and being very helpful! You both also have the greatness of awareness and thinking ahead to what may need to be done before we all leave."*

"Kim, you didn't complain or ignore me, instead you immediately did what I asked without disturbing anyone else in the group. Thank you for following directions."

The Nurtured Heart Approach is designed to help people tap into their own greatness: to see it, feel it, and be it. In his book *Playful Parenting*, Lawrence Cohen describes this as "filling the child's cup." Our psychological cups need to be filled with optimal nutrition, just like our drinking cups. By playing with a child; by creating ideal environments for them to play in; and by reflecting back to them their successes through the four recognition techniques of the Nurtured Heart Approach, you fill that cup.

Eventually, as you master these techniques, you'll learn to mix and match them and add your own creative flair. It is normal for them to feel awkward or challenging at first. If the child(ren) you are working with comment negatively or resist, just let them know that you've realized you would much rather talk about what is going well than what is going wrong, and that you want to give them credit for all the greatness they express even on an average day. Tell them, "You'll get used to it!" – and they will, even though the most resistant children will push back for some time to make sure that the old way of energy to negativity can't be reinstated. Even if that is far less pleasant, it is what feels familiar to them, and so they may do all they can to go back in that direction.

Acknowledgement Pointers

- **When you acknowledge a child in a group, do so in a way that every child in the group can hear it.** This helps everyone appreciate everyone else and know what behaviors will earn positive recognitions, and helps all children present understand your expectations and the rules.

- **Never give acknowledgements while a rule is being broken.** That calls for a reset (more on this below). You can dive back in with your acknowledgements as soon as you reset a child and he or she is no longer rule-breaking.

- **Be as detailed and precise as possible in your recognitions.** The more incontrovertibly true things you can say to the child about his or her success, the more impact you will have.

- **The giving of evidence** creates a sense of the child having a first-hand experience of being and having the qualities for which they are being appreciated. A child honored for respectfulness or kindness can take in a detailed compliment instead of feeling it as philosophical or theoretical – in a way where they feel it as not a question of whether they can or can't: they are living out that quality.

- **If a child resists acknowledgements,** simply say some variation on the following: "I see that these things I'm saying are making you uncomfortable. I've just been realizing that I tend to focus more on what goes wrong that what goes well. I am changing that. I know it feels weird right now, and I'm sure you'll get used to it soon enough!"

This Stand is totally aligned with play: being positive, being supportive, saying yes to someone's imaginative idea, saying yes to a suggestion, being in agreement, and being accepting of what is present in the moment. Play is so much about saying yes to possibilities.

The Nurtured Heart Approach is about seeing what is positive in each situation and recognizing it, acknowledging it, pointing it out, and celebrating it. All the recognition techniques work in this way, letting kids know that you see them profoundly, that you are aware of their feelings and needs. Again and again, we come back to this basic principle: that a primary need for all of us is to be seen and heard, appreciated and nourished, and to feel that we belong—that we are connected. This is the fuel we use to ignite the fire of greatness, and it is the cornerstone of saying absolutely yes to positivity.

Here is a story about Rythea Lee, a mom who decided to say Absolutely Yes to her child by following her lead completely.

Today I set an hour and a half to just focus on Torielle, my two-year old. I turned off phones, closed computers, and made sure I would have no distractions at all. I gave myself the task of following her lead on everything and not asking her to follow mine at all. Usually it's a back and forth, but I felt the need to empower her, to give her room to initiate completely for a while.

She put on her winter coat and kept it on for a half hour. Then, she led us to her dollhouse to put the 'baby' to sleep; to her wooden kitchen to eat a pretend birthday cake while she improvised a birthday song; and then she just wanted to stand together in the pantry for a little while. We drew with crayons for three minutes, then she put kid chairs in the middle of the room and had us sit on the chairs and fall off them in interesting ways. She pretended to be asleep and have me wake her up by blowing air on her face. She nursed for long periods (usually, I end it). She took my hand and led me around the house saying, "Come, Mama, come." She was very clearly thrilled to be getting my full attention compared to the usual routine of me breaking it up with phone calls and cooking and cleaning. After a while, we both entered a state of flow and ease. My nervous system went ahhhhh.

I know it is hard to find the time to do this, but I think even a half-hour a day of this kind of child-led play is huge for kids. They are almost always forced into adult agendas, timing, and ideas. I was surprised at how often I wanted to interrupt Torielle to tell her to go to the potty, or eat, or how much I wanted to suggest the play go in this direction or that. I had to let go of my agenda over and over again in order to give her room to lead us. Torielle did not push on my boundaries at all for the hour and a half, which for a two-year old, is kind of unheard of. I think it's because she felt so freed up. That's my theory, and I'm going with it.

Wow, it's raining outside, so let's watch a movie. Yes! Want to play a game of Monopoly? Yes! Want to play Freeze tag? Yes! Hey, let's pretend we are robots. Yeah, let's! How often can we say yes? It's not always possible, but it's possible more often for most of us.

The more children see that you are recognizing the positive in life, the more you are saying yes to their value, the more they will believe in it too. So the fuel that ignites the power of saying Absolutely Yes to the positive is the four recognition techniques of the Nurtured Heart Approach.

Play is a medium that breaks through the barriers of a difficult day or a bad mood and allows us to just be, in a playful way. The difficulties of the day can be left behind, along with frustrations, anger, or sadness. When I first start playing with a family, I do the majority of the acknowledging and energizing of what I see in each person that is positive or a success. I do this throughout the games, using short and quick acknowledgments. For example:

"As we were playing this game, I saw each of you laughing."

"Tim, I saw you working cooperatively with your sister and not letting go of her hand when the hula-hoop got to her, and when we were done, each of you stopped and turned your eyes to me. Thanks."

Once we finish the game, I will often ask the participants what they saw that was going right, or what it took for us to flow together and have fun. I say, "Let's take a few minutes to acknowledge each other and ourselves for what went right as we played this game."

As we play together more and more, the families I work with start to do this on their own. They will acknowledge each other while we are playing, without being prompted; or when we finish, they start to very naturally turn to one another and reflect on what was going well and what was successful. Each of them, from the youngest to the oldest, becomes more and more skilled at recognizing and noticing each other in an NHA way.

As I am playing with families, I use all four recognitions. If I am working with the family on a specific recognition, then I will be very intentional about using it to recognize each person. For example, I will check in with families every few weeks and ask them if there is a specific piece of the NHA on which they would like to focus in our next session. One family requested that we go over the four recognition techniques so that each of their children could learn them. The parents of this family had learned the approach prior to me coming into their homes (through counseling sessions and a parenting class) but their children hadn't. So for each of our next four sessions, we focused on one of the recognitions.

We started each session with a string-the-beads game, and then we shared successes. It is during this time of sharing successes that each child and parent is appreciated with a kind of emotional nutrition, through acknowledging themselves or being acknowledged by their child, sibling or parent, or myself. Once everyone had his or her "fill," we'd move on to the next piece – which, in this example, is one of the recognitions. We would take 10 minutes or so to go over the recognition for that week, keeping in mind that these children ranged from age five to 16 and I wanted all of them to be engaged and focused. This time went by quickly and we were on to playing. In my intro to the game, I let them know that I would be recognizing them during the game using Proactive Recognitions and that I might ask one of them to acknowledge someone else in this way. It's easy for everyone to get in the flow of positivity.

— **Valerie Potts,** *NHA therapist and trainer*

3. Absolutely Clear! I resolve to have clear rules and to give a consequence every time a rule is broken.

Games and play are great ways to emphasize the following of rules, and absolute clarity is very helpful in this regard. All of us love clarity, but children really thrive on it. It's a good feeling when we know what someone's boundaries are, and vice versa.

In play, there is sometimes a sense that perhaps there are no boundaries; everything is possible. Hang out with a preschooler and take part in their land of play; there are no boundaries; all things seem possible. As children grow older and become increasingly capable of holding more complexity, more challenge, and more engagement with others, delineating the rules and boundaries of a particular game is vitally important. The more clearly the rules are presented, the easier it is for the players to know the boundaries, and the smoother the experience flows for everyone. Absolute clarity creates a ground of safety and trust that allows greater enjoyment for the entire group, whether in play or in other social interactions.

Glasser likes to use a video game analogy to describe the way in which consequences are given in this approach. Intense children – even those who can barely sit still in a classroom or focus on a task – can play these games for hours with complete focus and absorption. The reason for this, Glasser states, is due to the perfect balance of energetic appreciation and recognition and consequences these games utilize, delivered in a manner that contradicts normal life. As long as the player is following the rules, points rack up and rewarding sounds and images stream in. Once a rule is broken, however, there is an immediate consequence or the game ends. The game doesn't give lectures or explain why the player lost. The game simply pauses. And all the player has to do to begin again is start over. At that juncture, the player has every possibility for success once again, with no residue from the past. Even though the consequences in the video game setting may appear drastic, in actuality the player is back in the game in seconds, ever more determined to not break the rules and to go to higher levels of success. The player absolutely has the sense of having crossed a line and of having had a consequence. Even though the short time out of the game was more of an illusion than a consequence of substance, 'game out/game off' had great impact because 'game-in/game-on' is so rich in energetic incentives. They can't wait to be back in the game, and following a time-out, they will usually bring with them more determination to not break the rules and to do better than ever.

Similarly, with the Nurtured Heart Approach, we use a quick, un-energized 'reset' in response to a broken rule. It constitutes a simple break from the action, a moment where energy stops passing from adult to child. It is followed, as quickly as possible, by a welcome-back to the action, which ends the reset. This should occur as soon as the adult can "accuse" the child of doing something right or NOT doing something wrong. This is not a punitive consequence; it is the truest form of time-out, where the child basically parses together the energetic meta-message: *"Reset yourself! Here's a chance to make a better choice."* And the adult intentionally, purposefully makes it his or her mission, when the rule-breaking stops, to express appreciatively that the child is *now not having* that issue that brought on the reset.

When a child breaks a rule, simply say, as calmly as possible (while still being audible), "[Child's name], reset." Just as you do with acknowledgements, do resets audibly enough for the whole room to hear, but do so unceremoniously without any prodding or explanation. Every time you reset one child in a group, the whole group can learn from it. It's not given with any edge or tone of frustration or anger; there's no shame in it; it isn't a punishment. It's a chance to pause, make a new choice, and get back into the game.

Be creative about resets. You can set up resets with groups of children ahead of time, saying that if they break a rule, they'll have to do a reset; and decide how it will look. Ultimately, the smoothest resets are right in the flow of the game. Just seconds later, you can appreciatively acknowledge new successes as they emerge, and the wisdom and kindness now being lived out by the child who is now following the rules.

All in all, a reset shouldn't take more than a few minutes, and optimally can be over in two seconds. If you stick with the truth of the moment, you can end the reset in the instant following the infraction if the child is now not breaking the rule. To end a reset, say the child's name again and remark upon whatever positive thing you see in that moment. "Natalie, I see you've done your reset successfully. You're now sitting quietly and not talking out of turn. Great restraint. I love that you're following that rule! You are back in the game." Or: "Christian, I love how you chose to take three deep breaths during your reset! That's the greatness of self-care."

♥ Time-In/Time-Out

The reset is, fundamentally, a time-out. If you have used time-outs unsuccessfully in your classroom or home, notice the differences between the NHA time-out and those you may have used in the past. It's brief, non-punitive, and low-energy. It does not require that the child move to a special chair or part of the room. Skilled practitioners can enact resets with enough creativity that the rule-breaking child can basically experience completing them, even if the child is intent on not being cooperative...with only positive results. If a child tries to escape a reset by going beneath a table, you might say after the child settles a bit, *"Isabella, I see you chose to take your reset under the table. You figured out what works for you. Beautiful creativity in figuring out how to take the time you needed."* You could use the same creativity with an older child running to her room and slamming her door. Wait until she emerges from her self-imposed exile – this will inevitably happen, and probably sooner than your fears might suggest, especially if you don't pursue her – and then, enthusiastically appreciate that she found a way to reset in her own good time. Point out how, at this time, she is brilliantly *not* breaking the rule she was breaking earlier. As much as you might be tempted to dredge up the past, stay with the truth of the moment and compliment the great choice she is currently making to be wise and in control.

By distinctly not energizing the negativity and by intently energizing the success of having completed the reset and now being within the scope of following the rules, the child is inexorably drawn into progressively more collaborative responses.

The real key to a time-out that works is a time-in that children don't want to miss out on! Stand Two creates that vibrant, fun, exciting, energetically compelling time-in. Time-out is void of relationship and boring in comparison, and children will be intrinsically motivated to follow the rules just to stay in time-in.

The Reset and the Stress Response

Game play can bring up emotions like anger, fear, and frustration, which can then trigger the natural adrenaline-fueled stress responses of fight, flight, or freeze – both for the players and for the adult trying to wrangle lots of excited kids. Anyone who's seen a player flip out on a referee or an overzealous parent making a fool of himself at a child's sporting event knows what this looks like.

Resetting is an extension of the basic advice to practice some form of initiating the relaxation response when we sense ourselves getting over-activated. A reset can include focusing on the breath; becoming mindful by noticing one's surroundings or body sensations; and focusing on what's going well in the next moment. For a young child, it may not be this complicated; all she knows is that she has to take a pause and make a new choice. For you, and for older children, the reset can encompass all we currently know – a lot! – about the value of mindfulness, emotional management, and positive communication. Kids of all ages get very proud and excited about their progressing ability to reset, especially under challenging circumstances.

The reset can be used to help yourself and others recognize when you, or they, are dropping into fear and negative reaction. When you ask someone to reset, you are asking him or her to come back to center – to a relaxed state of being – and to return to greatness. We create a growing proclivity toward success by pointing out the greatness that naturally arises through the child's next round of renewed choices. He or she is helped to grow in the greatness of skillful resetting.

The more we practice this in the context of play, where it's unlikely that any truly traumatic situation will transpire because of an overall playful atmosphere, the easier it will be to use this practice of resetting in response to bigger upsets and stresses outside the realm of play. As adults, we need to be able to reset ourselves: to come into our own balance and teach from that more centered place. We are resetting all the time anyway. How many times in a day do you falter, make a mistake, think self-critical or judgmental thoughts, or entertain worry or doubt? How many times a day do you find your way back to your baseline level of functioning? The truth is that resetting is inevitable and happening constantly. Now that you see this reality, have fun consciously conspiring to optimize it.

As kids experience the empowerment of resetting themselves, and in supporting others to do so, they are learning something crucial they might not have the chance to discover otherwise. This understanding is the foundation of emotional intelligence. Learning to reset directly supports development of executive function. Noticing your own stress response and witnessing it with some detachment is at the heart of mindfulness practice. Identifying anxiety, fear, and frustrations that occur on a daily basis, and then resetting back to harmony, is a form of mental competency that allows for numerous higher brain functions to emerge and strengthen. Taking some breaths, moving the body, playing, laughing, and seeking support if needed are all ways of shifting our energy back to more joyous possibilities. A reset is like a gift of renewal, keeping the play of life flowing smoothly and positively.

Since the last CTI (the Nurtured Heart Approach Certification Training Intensive), I use resets in a much broader way, in that they aren't only for misbehavior and negativity. I now use them anytime someone is distracted from the purpose at hand. For example: Let's say that while playing a game, Lisa is reminded of a story and starts to tell it. I would say, "Lisa, reset," and immediately bring my focus back to the game and the other participants. I would then acknowledge her by saying, "Lisa, you are no longer interrupting the game with your story. You reset yourself and are now being respectful of everyone and showing self-control, even though you were very excited to share your story. Thanks for completing that reset, and welcome back!"

It's as simple and quick as saying "Reset," then "Welcome back," and moving on. It barely interrupts the game, and the

> *child is motivated to get back into the fun of the game quickly.*
>
> - Valerie Potts

 Reset Pointers ——

- Only the person who gives the reset to the child can say when it has been completed. The child will eventually learn to recognize when he or she has successfully reset, but the adult should oversee that process and always give the reset a positive and appreciative closure.

- Saying the word 'reset' signals that the consequence has been issued; thanking the child for successfully completing the reset signals that the consequence has been successfully completed.

- Do not give positive acknowledgements (Stand Two) while the behavior you are resetting is ongoing. Wait for a shift.

- Avoid following a reset with any kind of commentary about the broken rule. If you must lecture the child about the rule, do so with regard to the child now following that rule, and talk about what that demonstrates about the child's greatness.

- Avoid warning children that *you're going to reset them if...!* Either the line has been crossed or it hasn't. If it hasn't, there is plenty to celebrate. If it has, it's a reset.

- Reset yourself often, as needed, any time you feel tempted to energize negativity. This sets a wonderful example for them and normalizes the reset as the standard consequence and a standard you adhere to. You might even encourage them to reset YOU when they think it might be needed.

Notching It Up

Whenever you feel the NHA isn't working, or it isn't working as well as you'd hope, *notch it up.* Apply the techniques with more gusto. Hold more tightly to the Stands. Get clearer about the rules and more rigorous about resetting. The answer is never to surrender any aspect of the Approach – indeed, any child who is challenging it is trying to ensure that you really mean business in terms of flipping upside-down energy right side up. Don't give the child any indication that you'll compromise on this front of celebrating their greatness rather than being critical. If you do, reset yourself, go back to the Stands, and get back in the game.

Play to Nurture Emotional Intelligence

Play offers a unique setting where kids can learn to support others in being okay with challenging feelings and to articulate their needs. The NHA is a great tool for moving through uncomfortable feelings, resetting, and getting back to greatness.

It can take adults some time to learn the difference between not giving energy to negativity and acknowledging a child's feelings. Feelings can be acknowledged in ways that are both positive and supportive: "Johnny, I see that you were upset during that game when Jack bumped into you. I could see you were getting angry, but you didn't push back or yell at him. That takes a lot of restraint and awareness, to not act out in anger. Thank you for resetting yourself and choosing to jump right back into playing the game."

We all know how important it is to feed our bodies the proper foods to grow and be healthy. Our emotional selves require optimal nutrition too. In the seminal work of Daniel Goleman and in his book, *Emotional Intelligence,* he argues that while IQ has gotten all the attention, our emotional quotient (or EQ) is equally, if not more, important. Games and play can bring up all kinds of emotions; this, in turn, brings many opportunities for acknowledgements of good emotional management, awareness of emotions, and willingness to vulnerably express emotions.

We all need inner resources to deal with the challenges and difficulties of life. We all need to learn how to reset ourselves back to our greatness and get ourselves back to feelings of happiness, gratitude, and harmony; and we all need to learn to cope with challenging feelings and to trust in our ability to return to a more balanced state (reset) when we feel overwhelmed.

Practice giving NHA recognitions in response to children's emotional management:

"Carla, I see you have a frustrated expression on your face, and I'm guessing that is because you don't yet understand the rules of the game we're about to play. I see you patiently re-focusing and trying to figure it out, and asking a friend quietly enough so that you don't interrupt me."

"Nathan, I am hearing that you don't want to participate today because you are feeling sad. Thanks for being willing to share that with me – it takes courage to admit to that feeling."

"Manuel and Tommy, you've clearly just shared seeing something that strikes you both as really funny! I can see you both want to burst out laughing loudly but you are being respectful by trying to keep it quiet and to keep the game going."

Nurtured Heart Play in a Time Where Play is Being Devalued

As schools eliminate playtime in favor of stronger academics – even for children in kindergarten and preschool! – educators lose out on opportunities to teach through play. Emphasis on academic outputs is squeezing out time for creativity, play, and recess in many school districts around the country.

The proliferation of technology and easily accessible media has also changed the playing field. More and more children are spending inordinate amounts of time inside and alone. This cultural shift away from physical, interactive play is most likely contributing to the kinds of behavior problems we see reaching epidemic proportions. We can refer to this as a play-deficit disorder, which goes hand in hand with what Richard Louv, author of *Last Child in the Woods,* has termed the nature-deficit disorder.

In schools, homes and programs, through skillful play leadership and using the Stands and Recognitions of the Nurtured Heart Approach, we can help bring nourishment and social-emotional skill building through play.

Play is a Great Way to Nurture Connection and Compassion

This work is based on the concept that we need to believe in the inherent goodness, the inherent greatness, of kids. When students feel engaged, safe, and included, they are more motivated to learn. When children feel open, present, and accepting of their own greatness, and that of others, it is easier for them to be cooperative, supportive, and kind.

Even in competitive sports where there is a great deal of emphasis on winning, the reality is that the core component of sports is teamwork, which is all about connection. The concept of good sportspersonship is all about empathy for the other players, including those on the other team—both in the thrill of victory and in the agony of defeat. Nurtured Heart Play helps kids to bridge that distance between themselves and the other players.

Neuroscience shows that when we observe empathetic behavior in someone else, the mirror neurons in the brain light up just as if we are experiencing the same emotions ourselves. We learn empathy by observing it in others and then trying out that behavior ourselves. Nurtured Heart Play is centered on helping participants to understand and experience the importance of interconnection and interpersonal awareness.

The other important piece is the knowledge that these don't have to be perfect relationships. We can all be insensitive, unaware, and emotionally clumsy at times, or just in a bad mood. In that case, we all get to practice the skills of tolerance and forgiveness. The Nurtured Heart Approach is a strategic methodology that supports everyone in clear communication and in resetting consistently to focus on strengths and successes.

Here is beautiful example of how the Nurtured Heart Approach can be used to support young children playing together, from NHA trainer and school counselor Stephanie Rule:

I took the kids out for an ice cream celebration Friday after school. After they finished their ice cream cones, they began playing in the play zone. At first they were the only kids in the play zone, and they were playing and enjoying themselves and each other so much! The then five-year-old, Josilyn, was playing WITH her little brother; she was playing honestly and fairly, including him in all her ideas, and welcoming his ideas as well. Because of the fact that I could not get in the play zone with the kids, I was walking all around the zone, kind of following them as they played. I was watching them intently and enjoying their cooperative, loving play. I saw so many opportunities to energize them for what they were doing right!

"Josilyn, I love the way you are not only including your brother in your play, but you are also allowing him to have his own ideas of what to do!"

"Evan, I see you playing with such kindness right now! You are not hitting your sister or pushing your sister, you are being so kind and loving with her!"

As I kept using NHA recognition techniques to give lots of these "drive-bys" to my kids, other kids started pouring into the play zone, which was exciting for Josilyn. She was happy to have older kids to play with. Now, with my two-year-old running around in this play zone where I cannot reach him and seeing seven older kids running around with him with very high energy, I was nervous that Evan would get hurt. So I pulled Josilyn out and gave her the first part of a Creative Recognition: "Josilyn, I need you to protect your baby brother in there. If he is going down the slide, I need you to tell the big kids to wait for your brother to be out of the way before they go down." Josilyn rose to that occasion better than I could have ever expected, and I poured on the positive recognitions. Josilyn kept her eye on her brother, stopped to help lift him up in a place he couldn't, and continued to include him in the game that she was playing with the older kids! At one point, Evan was wandering around looking for his big sister, and she came and found him and continued to include him in their games. With all these kids running around and playing in the play zone, it had become very loud in there. Still, I continued to energize my kids for the greatness they were demonstrating: playing kind and fair, being considerate of all the other kids around, protecting each other, and all the while being respectful of the rules.

When it was time to stop playing and go home, I did not have one single issue! Both Josilyn and Evan were very respectful and made responsible choices to stop playing right

> *away, get their shoes back on, and walk out without any whining or complaining. I know this was directly related to my use of NHA as they played that day.*

The story shows how Stephanie took an active role in a busy play situation to create a vibrant time-in that made good choices extremely rewarding for her children. She stayed engaged with her children and gave them frequent reminders of their inherent value while they played. Inner wealth was built and fun was had by all.

The Importance of Physical and Emotional Safety

Creating an atmosphere of *safety* and *freedom* is vital for true play to happen. In fact, the special state of mind characteristic of playfulness happens only when there is a zone of safety: where the rules feel fair and where experimentation with new ideas and skills feels safe. An adult presence is sometimes needed during play to ensure that this atmosphere is created. This being said: children can and should play by themselves, too. Leaving children to their own devices is important for their development of independence, creativity, and social-emotional learning, and is also very useful for giving parents or teachers a break so they can rest or finish their work. Leaving a group of children alone lets them work things out on their own, which builds their communication skills and creativity. Jay Giedd, a neuroscientist at the University of California, has stated, "The trouble with over-structuring is that it discourages exploration." One point of balance is to check in now and then during independent play with the pure intention of giving appreciative commentary.

Glasser likes to say that we are never too busy for a problem. We always show up fully for issues, no matter how distracted by other urgencies we claim to be. The key to progressing inner wealth is 'flipping' that mindset to make a few minutes here and there to point out successes.

The nature of play is free and spontaneous and therefore potentially chaotic, which is usually not the atmosphere that teachers want to create in a classroom. How do we maintain that balance of spontaneity, freedom, creative expression, fun and safety? How do we foster spontaneity and freedom, embrace the unpredictable nature of play, and still have an enjoyable, productive experience as teachers and caretakers? By mastering the art of playfulness...and by using the techniques employed in the Nurtured Heart Approach.

CHAPTER TWO

NHA
PLAY LEADERSHIP:
PRACTICAL MATTERS

Beyond the application of Nurtured Heart principles and techniques to game play with groups of children are the logistics of game leadership. A few general guidelines are provided here so that you don't have to reinvent that wheel, and so you can focus on nurturing the hearts of your players.

Enrolling Resistant Players

Children are easy to enroll, but some teens are well on their way to being adults who are afraid to play. When they hear the word "play," they think of competition, winning, and losing, and for those who don't enjoy such things, play doesn't sound like any fun at all; or, they may see play as something that is too childish for them or even stressful in terms of making a concerted effort to get along.

Most people will gladly risk being playful and silly when they feel safe, but it is vital to be patient with those who aren't ready to stretch in this way. Your job is to establish a safe, nonjudgmental space and facilitate the growth of a community where participants can cut loose. Given the high-pressure environments within which many of us live and work, it is a relief for many adults and children alike to experience a place where games are meant to be about fun rather than winning/losing. These games and exercises are designed to help everyone not only appreciate, but also help facilitate inclusiveness. One teacher calls these cooperative games "exercises for the heart." Creating a safe container for exploration is your responsibility, and your privilege. Create an environment where mistakes are okay, silliness is very okay, and fun equals success.

Be aware of any anxiety and resistance that may come up for anyone. From time to time, ask the players to take a moment and notice how they are feeling. Adding in Nurtured Heart Recognitions throughout a play session helps everyone to feel safe and connected. For example, "I noticed everyone was laughing and taking care of each other during that last game." Or, "I noticed a lot of creativity when we were playing, and everyone was listening and being patient and waiting for your turn." Or, "I like how well you were able to keep your kindness and fun going during that game, even though you seemed frustrated."

If a game entails some level of silliness from a more reserved group, specifically address this. Ask inviting questions like, "Are you ready to get a little crazy?" or "Are you willing to laugh at your own mistakes?" This will set the tone for nonjudgmental fun and alert all participants that they are invited to let their guard down in order to fully enjoy it.

General Guidelines

- Plan ahead. Make a list of the games before you launch into the session. Keep it close at hand throughout.

- Practice leading games before you bring them to a group – even if you only do so mentally. Work out the language and the transitions in your mind before getting in front of others to lead.

- Games that you like most, that you know best, and that you can convey with clarity and enthusiasm should be the heart of your repertoire. Experiment with new games somewhere in the middle of your line-up. Start strong and end strong.

- Once you are more experienced and know several games, you can be more flexible. Plan, but be open and sensitive to the vibe of the youth with whom you are working and take their lead. If their energy is low, maybe you'll want to bring a more energizing, physical game; if they're already highly energetic, a more mellow game might fit. Or you might choose to "go with the skid" and play a game that is more matched to the existing mood in the room. As you develop these skills, you will learn to read students and bring what will work best.

Game Sequencing

Depending on how you use NHA Play, you may only play one game at a time – say, to take a break from academics or as a warm-up for another planned activity in an after-school program. For a longer play session for a group of youth, a sequence like this will work beautifully:

1. Simple icebreaker

2. Large-group name game

3. A game that entails the group working in smaller circles

4. Partner games

5. More challenging games (as everyone gets more warmed up)

6. Sillier, more animated games as everyone gets more loosened up!

7. Closing appreciation/acknowledgement/greatness circle

At the end of a session, always leave time to debrief Nurtured Heart style with a greatness circle or an appreciation circle. A few ideas for the final circle:

- Ask for appreciations from participants to other participants.

◉ Ask for each participant to share one thing they learned about their own greatness by playing one of the games.

◉ Have each participant turn to a neighbor in the final circle and spend half a minute making energizing statements; then have the pair switch so both can hear these statements.

◉ As the teacher, give several greatness recognitions to participants – both as individuals and as a group. Have the rest of the group make a certain signal or gesture you designate to mean "I agree!" – as in, "I agree with this statement about the other person's greatness!" if they see that greatness too: a quiet snapping of the fingers, the American Sign Language sign for "I agree" ('nodding' a closed fist up and down), or a 'golf clap' (very quiet) will work; or dream up your own signal.

Transitions Between Games

Enter with enthusiasm and playfulness. Be inviting, open, and clear. When working with new groups – even when leading play trainings with adults – it is important to realize that many people have had bad experiences with traditional sports or standard modes of play, either in school or at home. From the beginning, emphasize the non-competitive nature of these games, and affirm that together, we are all creating a sense of safety. It's always all about the players feeling supported, included, and valued.

Whenever possible, it is recommended to start in a circle to create a sense of the group as a whole. In a large group (about 30 or more), it is good to begin with an energizer, then move into some big circle games that let players learn about each other. Name games are always important, but in large groups they can take a long time, so it is good to do a few energizers before a name game to make sure everyone is engaged. If you are working with a lot of people, you may wish to break them into pairs and small groups after a few circle games to promote closer interactions.

Over time, work on smooth transitions between games, where you are able to move from game to game, divide the class into small groups or pairs, or re-convene into a large group with minimum chaos. Avoid lag time where players are uncertain of what to do. When games require partnering up, avoid saying simply, "Choose a partner." Count off by threes or fours around the circle and then hold fingers up; or get really creative, finding ways to create groups based on birthdays, heights, or favorite numbers, or even how many times participants have been to Disneyland!

For example: after a large group game, have the whole group pause, then put up one, two, or three fingers; then, each person finds two others who held up the same number of fingers to form a group of three for the next game. (Adjustments can be made if the groups are uneven.)

Or use mindfulness as a bridge between games. Try inviting players to walk mindfully around the room between games, noticing any sounds, smells, or other sensations in their bodies: After a game involving three people per group, have the whole group break apart and mill around the room in a slow walk. Play around with different body awareness cues: "Imagine there is a string from the ceiling gently pulling upward on the top of your head. Notice how that feels. Now walk as though you're hurrying to catch an airplane.... Now freeze. The person closest to you is your partner. Spread out in pairs around the room." Be sure to consistently energize participants for collaboration and creativity!

Transitions are a good time to share recognitions and other positive observations.

• "I notice you are ready for the next game to start; you are looking at me with focus and a cooperative attitude that I appreciate. Thanks."

• You could have been disturbing your friends in the transition between these two games; instead, you were patient and immediately formed a circle when I asked."

• "Thank you all for being flexible with the process."

Teaching Games: Guidelines

Use the acronym DDADA to help teach the rules and objectives of each game:

- **Describe** the activity.

- **Demonstrate** the activity: A quick demonstration helps visual and kinesthetic learners.

- **Ask** questions: Ask everyone if they understand. Re-clarify if anyone is at all confused.

- **Do** it: Start playing the game as quickly as possible. If the descriptions and demonstrations are too long players will get bored.

- **Adapt** it: If something isn't working, stop, re-clarify the rules if necessary, and suggest some changes; or ask the group for some suggestions as to how to change the game to fit everyone's needs.

Maximum Activity Plan (MAP)

Another very important concept to keep everyone active, engaged, and represented in the acronym **MAP: Maximum Activity Plan**. A game with a good MAP fully involves as many of those present as possible.

Kickball does not have a good MAP. One person kicks and runs and usually one or two fielders get involved, but everyone else is just standing around watching. This can also be an issue with large circle games. For example, if a circle game involving 30 people has only one person as "It," and if that person just points at one person at a time, there are a lot of people just watching. You can enhance the MAP of this game by adding an extra "It" or two (or three or four!) once the game gets going and everyone understands how it works.

Tag games where everyone is moving naturally have great MAPs. But there are still a few guidelines with these games to maximize engagement. Balance the number of "Its" with the number of players: a standard rule of thumb is to have one "It" per ten players. Also keep in mind the size of your playing field. For a running tag game, setting the boundaries too close can make the game too crowded and potentially unsafe; if they are too far apart, there is too much running and not enough playful interaction.

Getting A Group's Attention

A happy, boisterous group of youth can sometimes lose focus. A microphone is helpful with large groups, but if you don't have one, don't despair! Try these tricks for re-focusing groups in positive ways:

- Raise your hand and wait silently for a few beats, looking around. Youth will start to imitate you; as soon as that happens, give positive acknowledgements. Before you know it, everyone in the room will have a hand in the air, waiting for further instruction.

◉ Or you can say, "If you hear the sound of my voice, clap once." (Some kids will clap.) "If you hear the sound of my voice, clap twice." (More kids will join in.) "If you hear the sound of my voice, clap three times." (By this point, everyone will be re-focused on you.) Remember to energize compliance and be creative! You might try another version where youth shout out the word "Greatness!'"

◉ Another way is to try a call-and-response re-focusing tactic, where a lyric from a popular song is used. One teacher working with a group of teens would shout out, "I wear my grandpa's clothes"—a line from the Macklemore song "Thrift Shop" – and the response would be, "You look incredible." It's pretty cool to hear seventy teenagers shout this back to you!

◉ Reset part of the group or even the entire group. For example: "Right now, I'm going to reset myself and everyone who is still having a conversation." Then, as soon as the reset occurs, make it your mission to appreciatively express gratitude for the shift to collaborative readiness. This is most in keeping with the pure version of the Nurtured Heart Approach. Many people working with even large groups quickly discover that after the first request for attention, this is the simplest and purest way to get back to play.

Whatever techniques you choose to re-focus, be patient, clear, and positive. Allow the group to slowly become focused and quiet.

❦ NHA Play and Recess

For many children, recess is a time to let loose and play freely. For other kids, recess can mean bullying, exclusion, and mean-spirited competition. Schools embracing NHA in more encompassing ways see great changes in this regard; but in general, educators are too busy or overwhelmed with other responsibilities to oversee and facilitate positive play experiences on the playground. Because free, interactive play has become a diminished part of the average childhood, kids may not arrive at school with the skills required to play fairly, creatively, and imaginatively when given total freedom to do so. The NHA is a wonderful tool for supporting the development of those skills during recess time.

When I first began my job, I was charged to train all the teachers in the school to utilize the Nurtured Heart Approach in the classroom. However, the recess monitors were not a part of that initial training. Students were still running into problems during recess, so I did Nurtured Heart training for these monitors – and this has totally changed the environment at recess! As yard monitors focus on children's successes, everyone is enjoying recess more.

I also empowered a number of students and yard monitors to be "Greatness Detectives" whose job is to seek out evidence of greatness during recess. They write this evidence on slips of paper and give them to those students, who love getting these "Greatness Passes."

-Vivian Barajas

Nurtured Heart Play in Therapeutic Settings

Howard Glasser shares that when he first began to teach the NHA to interns at the Center for the Difficult Child – the counseling center he opened in Tucson – they quickly became as effective as or more effective than therapists with much more experience using traditional methods. Therapists and school counselors have flocked to learn the NHA and apply it to their clinical practices or to their work in schools. It is a very common practice to integrate play into therapeutic approaches and therapeutic settings for children, such as group homes and residential treatment centers. Adding the Nurtured Heart Approach to play-focused therapy can be of immense support to children and families.

Safety First

Your first priority should always be making a game physically and emotionally safe. As you introduce the session, advise the players that some of the activities could be challenging, and encourage them to embrace challenges with a playful spirit. Encourage them to stay aware of their feelings but stretch themselves into that potential discomfort. Players should always feel free to choose their own level of participation. As we try to nurture healthy self-awareness and a collaborative, considerate mind/body connection in others, we must trust the self-knowledge they bring with them. Part of creating a safe environment is setting a nonjudgmental tone not only toward mistakes, but also towards opting out.

CHAPTER THREE

GREAT GAMES:
AN INTRODUCTION

You have to go back to ancient Greece and see nothing has really changed. We either sit around the fire and tell stories or play games. These are the two activities that are basically profound and alluring to the human spirit.

— George Lucas

In Nurtured Heart Play, we combine stories and play: within the context of guided games, we have opportunities to tell stories about the greatness of the people who are playing.

— Howard Glasser

In the following chapters are a number of our favorite games for Nurtured Heart Play. We have broken them up into four easy sections: Energizers, Active Games, Improv Theater Games, and Mindfulness Games. The book culminates with Greatness Games, a few activities that focus simply on seeing and acknowledging greatness in self and others.

Beyond what is offered in these pages, there are hundreds of great energizers, cooperative games, theater games, songs, dances, and movement activities from which to choose. Perhaps you'll feel inspired to create your own games. Once you see how the Nurtured Heart Approach dovetails with play, you will be able to discern how any collaborative game can be taken to the level of greatness.

In the Resources section, we provide some of our favorite places to gather more tools for your tool kit. Ultimately, that is what matters: expanding your capacity to engage with kids through play, providing optimal emotional and energetic nutrition for those around you and for yourself, and taking a moment to reset yourself to greater playfulness when necessary.

We follow this format in most chapters covering specific games:

1. Materials: if supplies are needed, they are listed in this section; if none are needed, this section is left out.

2. Set Up: what supplies are needed, how many players the game is suited to, and how to give participants the information they'll need to dive into game play.

3. SEL Skills: SEL is *social-emotional learning.* The Collaborative for Social-Emotional Learning (CASEL) defines SEL as "the process through which children and adults acquire and effectively apply the knowledge, attitudes, and skills necessary to understand and manage emotions, set and achieve positive goals, feel and show empathy for others, establish and maintain positive relationships, and make positive decisions" (www.casel.org). Integrating SEL into any program is a welcome recognition of what, intuitively, every NHA proponent or practitioner already knows: that learning best happens in the context of supportive relationships; and that whatever a student's academic or athletic achievements might be, real happiness and contentment in life come through healthy, positive relationships. CASEL defines five core SEL competencies: self-management, self-awareness, social awareness, relationship skills, and responsible decision-making. In these pages, we chose not to limit ourselves to naming these specific competencies as supported or taught through game play. Instead, we listed what we call "SEL Skills" we believe are being reinforced.

4. Game On: a numbered list of steps for game play.

5. Look for Greatness: a list of suggested behaviors/choices to energize during and after game play.

6. Clarity for Players: a list of rules for game play to serve as ideas for where to reset or give Proactive Recognitions (when the rules are being followed).

7. Variations: variations on the game being described.

8. Ideas for Reflection: suggestions for post-game discussion and de-brief, designed to highlight positive choices and give opportunities to recognize and be recognized in greatness.

CHAPTER FOUR

ENERGIZERS:
THE GREATNESS OF GROUP ENERGY

Energizers lighten the mood and pick up the energy of the group. They are ideal ice-breakers for groups new to one another or for starting out a group games session or class period. Really, any of the games in this book will be effective in shifting energy; we chose the games here because they are easy to explain and simple to play. Active play can get underway without much preparation.

 **Gotcha**

Set Up

This game works for 10-30 players.

Have everyone stand in a circle.

Have players hold their left hands out, palm up, and their right hands up with index finger pointed upward.

Have all players drop their right index finger into the left palm of the person to their left.

The leader then explains that at the call of the word, "Gotcha," everyone will try to pull their right index finger up and away from their neighbor's left palm, while at the same time trying to grab the finger that is touching their left palm.

This game is a great opener: simple, active, and exciting.

SEL Skills

- Relationship skills

- Social awareness

- Managing stress

- Focus

- Emotional regulation

Game On

1. The leader shouts out the word "Gotcha," and everyone reacts.

2. The leader then asks the players to reset back to the starting position and play continues.

3. Try switching the direction of the hands: right palm up, left finger into the neighbor's right palm.

4. The leader can choose other players to call out the "Gotcha."

Look for Greatness
Energize:

- Maintaining focus and rules while being competitive.

- Being aware and in control of emotions when there is excitement and anticipation.

- Resetting easily back to readiness to play.

- Safety and respect of other player's bodies.

- Attention to prompting from the leader and being very responsive with the body.

- Cultivating the fun of the excitement through positivity.

◉ Willingness to embrace a challenge.

Clarity for Players

No touching during the game in a disruptive or disrespectful manner.

No disrupting your teammates in the circle from getting ready for each round.

No arguing, roughhousing, bad words, or breaking any other of the general classroom rules while we are playing.

Let the players know that you trust them to follow the rules of the game as well as the general class rules; and that, if necessary, you will reset them so they can get right back into the game.

Variations

You can play this game in pairs; just have the players face each other and repeat the above directions.

You can make a specific number or word the cue for action; for example, the number three, or the word "potato." If you use a number, get tricky with tossing out numbers to fool participants: "One... two... four... eight... twelve... THREE!"

Using a word means you tell a story in which the word will occur: for example, potato. "Once I went out to dinner at this new restaurant. They had a lot of foods that started with 'p.' They had pasta...they had persimmons...they had parsnips... and of course, one of my favorites, pozole...and I ended up ordering one sad little POTATO!" These options are fun for student volunteers to lead as well.

Ideas for Reflection

Encourage group members to give one or two recognitions to self and/or others participating about what they observed or appreciated:

- "What was great about what you observed or experienced?"

- "Is there anything you might do to notch it up next time?"

This game plays with the concept of multitasking, doing two things at once. Focus, concentration, readiness and anticipation are all required.

- "How did it feel to anticipate the call for action, the gotcha moment? Did you have success? If not, why?"

Connect this lesson to life: In this game, there is really nothing at stake, but it still feels like a test, similar to coming up to bat in baseball or getting ready to play in a concert.

- "How do you handle the excitement of anticipation in your day-to-day life?"

- "How do you reset yourself after you've become anxious?"

- "Can you think of instances in everyday life where you need to reset and move on? What does it take to do that? What are some examples of your successes in doing that, today or at other times?"

- "What are some good strategies you can use in the future to deal with the stress or fear of anticipation and excitement?"

End the game and reflection time by acknowledging the group for their exceptional participation.

Greatness Flows for Anyone Who...

Set Up

This game works well for 10-30 players.

Set up chairs for all participants in a large circle.

Explain to everyone that statements will be made using the beginning phrase, "Greatness flows for anyone who..." and that, if it includes them, they will get up and safely move to another chair.

Statements can choose to highlight a sense of community and commonality by showing points of connection between participants. Even those students who might feel isolated and like they have nothing in common with their classmates, or that they have unique backgrounds, ethnicities, or ideals, may well find more closeness with their peers and shared greatnesses.

SEL Skills

- Relationship skills

- Social awareness

- Self-management

Game On

1. Game play begins with everyone seated in a large circle.

2. Explain that one person will stand in the center of the room and state something that is true about him or herself.

3. The leader gives an example by going first. "Greatness flows for anyone who_____." (...who has owned a pet... who has two sisters...who likes rainy weather...who has been to Ohio....it can be anything that is true for you.)

4. Instruct others for whom this same thing is true to stand up in the circle.

5. After the person in the center acknowledges those who've stood ("Thank you for taking the risk to be honest and revealing"), each person standing moves quickly and safely to a new seat.

6. Whoever is left without a chair goes to the center of the circle for the next round to create his or her twist on "Greatness flows for anyone who..."

7. Tell students if someone else sits in a seat they wanted, it will be an opportunity to show their greatness by graciously finding another seat.

8. Take time occasionally to recognize the group for qualities you wish to appreciate: their cooperation, respect for safety, kindness, or other great qualities. For example: "I didn't see anyone pushing or shoving. You all quietly walked and respected the space of others. That makes me feel confident I could prompt you to cross the room in some creative way and you would do it safely. Thank you for acting responsibly." Do this as often as you can without disrupting the forward movement of the activity.

Look for Greatness

Energize:

- Close listening and attention to the leader.

- Bodily safety.

- Enthusiasm in bursts of action.

- Being the center of attention and letting personality and

individuality be seen by the group.

- Openly sharing about interests, strengths, points of gratitude, fears, and preferences.

- Encouraging other players and helping them to succeed or feel welcome in sharing.

- Creative prompts to engage deeply other players' sense of claiming who they are.

- Joyfulness, kindness and friendship towards peers as they reveal who they are.

- Playfulness.

- Agility.

- Sensitivity to others, meaningful interactions, supportiveness, and mindful ways of collaborating.

Clarity for Players

No bumping, pushing, kicking, shoving or fighting for a chair.

No disrespectful or rude words or actions.

No side talking or distracting self or others.

Let players know that you have faith they will be able to follow the rules of the game as well as the general class rules; and that, if necessary, you will reset them so they can get right back into the game.

Variations

Give students a category to consider. A few examples: foods, music, hobbies, sports, weather, animals, vacation spots, and special skills.

Tell students you will be giving them a new way to move from one seat to another. Creatively select movement options based on your group's mobility, age, and skill level. Examples: dancing to the next seat, jumping, using swimming motions, hopping, applauding their way, smiling their way, moving with a grumpy expression, or moving in slow motion.

Guide students to more meaningful lead-ins. Examples: "Greatness flows for anyone who...has said something to make someone feel encouraged" or "...has seen kindness in someone else today" or "...has seen their own greatness today in something they did." The latter can lead to wonderful shares and appreciations.

Attempt to move into deeper realms of connection such as feelings, dreams, personal strengths, points of gratitude, qualities of greatness, goals, and life challenges.

Creating connections with Word-Shares can be a fun sidebar. They can be related to the question just asked. For example, give those standing a chance to briefly respond to prompts such as: "What kinds of pets have you owned?" or "What are the names of some of the pets you've had?" Give these prompts when people have stood to show that whatever the person in the center has said is true for them as well, before the group switches chairs.

Ideas for Reflection

Encourage group members to give one or two recognitions to self and/or others participating about what they observed or appreciated. Create momentum for this by modeling as needed. Example: "I am so impressed by how creative our class was with the statements. It really helped us connect and learn more about each other. You all showed courage to share and that is a great quality I see in you."

Ask the group for creative ideas for questions and movements across the circle for the next time you play the game. Be sure to provide appreciations for this brainstorming of ideas.

Save some time to sit with the group to talk about such things as:

- "What commonalities of greatness did we find in each other?"
- What surprised you about your fellow players?"
- "What were your favorite parts of the game?"

Connecting the lesson to their lives:

- "How does it affect you when your peers don't know that much about you?"
- "How does learning about your peers change how you feel about them?"
- "Can you think of an example where learning about someone's likes and interests helped you to feel more connected to them?"
- "How does learning about you change the way you might treat one another?"

Remind students of the qualities identified at the start of the lesson. Did they see what they predicted? Model recognizing students with strong appreciation and acknowledgment.

- "I am really impressed by how insightful your answers have been. It really shows how present and thoughtful you were being during the game!"
- "I got to see that you all were excited to let your classmates see something new about who you are. You all wanted to learn truthfully about each other and listened attentively."

- Support the conversation by asking what qualities they saw in others, in themselves and in the group as a whole. End the game and reflection time by acknowledging the group for its participation.

Happy/Great/Love

Set Up

Divide players into groups of three.

Demonstrate the following three symbols/gestures:

1. Shiny Happy Person, performed with hands placed on joyful hearts and the happy sound of, "Wheeeee!"

2. Greatness-Activated Person, who shoots sparks of greatness out of their heart with fingers spread wide, making the sound "Ptchooo! Ptchooo!"

3. Loving and Passionate Person, who blows kisses with both hands, making kissing sounds.

SEL Skills

- Relationship skills

- Social awareness

- Cooperation

- Focus

- Visualization

- Imagination

Game On

Each group of three stands with backs facing in.

Tell them, "Tune into to your group. Who are you all together? As you tune into your group, imagine one of the symbols in your mind."

"On the count of three... Turn and make the gesture you have visualized!"

Ask the group, "Who was connected?" (Meaning, in which groups did the same gesture come through all three people?)

Do three rounds.

At the end, ask which groups were connected at once, twice, and three times.

Look for Greatness

Energize:

- Making an effort to experience connection and cooperation.

- Attuning with other people.

- Emotional and intuitive intelligence that helps players match each other.

- Immense power of visualization that exudes from imagining one of the symbols.

- Willingness to work together to create success and take care of each other.

- Choosing joy and playfulness in the process of agreement, anticipation and achievement.

- Finding fun in missing the mark.

- Creativity in creating the symbols and movements.

- Being in tune with personal emotions, and physical and intellectual experiences in the course of playing with others.

- Taking care of one's self.

Clarity for Players

No talking when instructions are given.

No preplanning with your partners about which symbol you are going to do.

Let the players know that you trust them to follow the rules of the game as well as the general class rules; and that, if necessary, you will reset them so they can get right back into the game.

Variations

Play with different symbols – for example, Elves, Giants, and Wizards.

Have the players brainstorm to create their own symbols that represent Happiness, Greatness and Love.

Form larger groups and have them develop three simple, interactive statues that represent something – either the themes of Happiness, Greatness, and Love, built from individuals in each group, or some other set of three themes; then, have all the groups play the game together, with each group as a team that sees whether it can intuitively match the other groups on the count of three.

Ideas for Reflection

Take a moment during the game to allow the group to share appreciations and recognitions to each other: "What qualities of greatness are we witnessing during the playing of this game?"

Offering simple prompts will help create structure for this sharing:

- "What is making this game work well?"

- "What qualities of greatness are you noticing being expressed during the game?"

Happy/Great/Love is a playful way for the players to make physical expressions of the happiness, greatness, and lovingness. It is amazing how simple gestures can help to elicit those feelings in the body:

- "How did it feel in your body when you did the various expressions?"

- "How did the gestures give off energy of happiness, greatness and love? Is it helpful to physically express your happiness, or your greatness, or love in life?"

Another key element in this game is this sense of attunement. Explore with the players what it felt like to tune into their group:

- "Did you feel there was connection, or a felt sense of what symbols your group members might do?"

- "When I asked you to visualize one of the symbols, did you get that picture in your mind? Did that help you to tune into your group?"

- "What did you tell yourself or do internally that helped make the external match-up happen?"

Connect the lessons to life:

- "Where is it helpful to sense what someone else is feeling or thinking... a mother taking care of a baby? Are there times when it is helpful to be able to imagine or visualize something- maybe when determining what you want to accomplish in an endeavor."

Remind students of the qualities identified at the start of the lesson. Model by recognizing them with strong appreciation and acknowledgment:

- "I am really impressed with the way everyone focused and tuned into their group. I really noticed the enthusiasm and excitement when you matched with your group. That shows the intention and desire to match, and the cooperative and engaged spirit that you all have."

End the game and reflection time by acknowledging the group for its participation.

Have You Ever?

Set Up
This game works well for 6-20 players.

Players sit in a circle on chairs or on something else to designate their space (a pillow or jacket).

Go to the center of the circle to will start the game; at least, proceed this way the first time your group plays the game. In the future, if you play again, a student can begin because the group will already know how to play.

SEL Skills

- Relationship skills
- Social awareness
- Focus
- Self-regulation

Game On

1. Go to the center of the circle.

2. Say your name; have the group shout out, "Hi, [your name]!"

3. Then, say "Have you ever..." and finish with something you have done or experienced: for example, "Have you ever broken a bone?"

4. Explain that everyone else who has broken a bone – for whom the answer to the question is "yes" – should immediately and safely cross the circle and find another chair.

5. In the mix, the person in the middle also attempts to find an open seat. The player who does not get a seat is the next person in the middle and asks the next question.

6. Call out/appreciate qualities of greatness that you witness in the course of play.

Look for Greatness

Energize:

- Seeking and highlighting common experiences through questions.

- Building community by helping everyone to feel included, seen, and heard.

- Sharing truths about one's self with honesty, reverence, and gaiety.

- Helping other players to enjoy sharing with appropriate and fun questions.

- Enjoying the physical energy.

- Responding promptly to the leader.

- Enthusiastically participating.

- Supporting others' emotional safety by modeling self-respect and appreciation.

Clarity for Players

No bumping, pushing, kicking, shoving or fighting for a chair.

No disrupting your teammates in the circle in ways that prevent them from getting ready for each question.

No inappropriate questions or questions that might cause embarrassment.

No arguing, roughhousing, or bad words, or breaking any other of the general classroom rules while we are playing.

Let the players know that you trust them to follow the rules of the game as well as the general class rules; and that, if necessary, you will reset them so they can get right back into the game.

Variations

Sometimes players get stuck when they have to think of a question on the spot. Recommend specific question categories, and emphasize that the question can be about *anything* that person has *ever* done (within bounds of appropriateness for the setting, of course). "Have you ever brushed your teeth?" is fair game, as is "Have you ever eaten chocolate ice cream?" or "Have you ever traveled to another state?"

With younger children, the teacher may actually ask the questions or be in the middle and help the middle player think of a question.

You can add an element of connection between those who have had the same experience as the person in the center; for example, everyone can be asked to give three high-fives on the way through the middle of the circle to their new seat.

A variation for younger children is described in "The Cool Breeze Blows for Anyone Who..."

Ideas for Reflection

Encourage group members to give one or two recognitions to self and/or others participating about what they observed or appreciated.

- "I am so impressed with how playful and enthusiastic everyone was during the game, and how much respect you showed to each other."

- "Is there anything you might do next time to notch this game up?"

This game is all about feeling into a sense of a shared experience. It takes focus, concentration, and listening to play this game. So some questions focusing on these qualities can be supportive of the social-emotional learning that is taking place during the playing of the game.

- "How did it feel to learn new things about your friends?'

- "Did you learn anything new that surprised you?"

- "Do you feel that you know your friends better now after this game? Do you feel closer to them?"

- "What else did you see happen while we were playing?"

- "Was everyone being safe with each other?"

- "What qualities of greatness were being expressed? And what was the evidence of that?"

- "What was making the game work well?"

- "What would you notch up about the game to make it even better?"

- "How did it feel to be in the center and have all the attention on you?"

- "How did it feel when everyone really listened to you?"

Connect the lesson to life:

- "How do you make new friends? Do you share your likes and experiences with them? Do you ask them questions to get to know them better?"

- "Who and where in life is it important to ask questions to get to know someone?"

- "What are some examples of your successes in asking questions and listening, today or at other times? What qualities does it take to be a good listener and asker of questions?"

Support the conversation by asking what qualities they saw in others, in themselves and in the group as a whole.

End the game and reflection time by acknowledging the group for its participation.

Introduce a New Friend in Greatness

Set Up

This game is played in pairs and then in a circle.

Have the players find partners – someone whom they have not met before or do not know well. Have pairs either sit in a circle or spread out to promote better listening between partners.

Give the pairs a few minutes to tell each other a few things they would like other people to know about their lives: accomplishments, hobbies, favorite sports teams, favorite music, favorite books, family members, pets. Have the group talk as much as possible about their qualities of greatness. What do they feel they are good at? What are their strengths?

Then, have the group sit either in a large circle or audience-style to take turns introducing their new friends.

SEL Skills

- Relationship skills

- Social awareness

- Focus

- Connection

- Active Listening

- Concentration

- Optimism

Game On

1. Have the players begin sharing and give them a few minutes to connect and rehearse what they are going to say about their partners.

2. Have players gather back into a circle. The pair chosen to start stands, and each tells the group a few of the interesting things he or she has learned about his or her new friend. For example: "This is my new friend Sue. She is really good at soccer and she also loves to spend time with her family eating chocolate ice cream."

3. The person introduced stands and bows as the group applauds and cheers.

4. The other partner can then sit down or remain standing to be introduced by his or her partner.

5. If the players are used to speaking about qualities of greatness, introduce the game as "My Partner's Greatness," listed in the variation below. If this is new to your group, have them play the simpler version the first time. After becoming more comfortable with the appreciations and acknowledgements of NHA, they can play the notched-up version of this game.

Look for Greatness
Energize:

- Being focused on listening closely and building community.

- Making it fun and inviting to share and empathizing by truly hearing someone else's story.

- Helping someone to feel special by appreciating how they choose to express their greatness, and reflecting it back to them.

- Skilled mental recollection when remembering what the partner shared.

- Bravely speaking up in front of others.

- Kindly and sensitively sharing what their partner said.

- Connecting with confidence, willingness, and love.

Clarity for Players

No being disruptive while players are sharing.

No making fun of anyone's introduction of his or her friend.

No arguing, bad words, or breaking other general rules of the class-room.

Let players know that you trust them to follow the rules; and that, if necessary, you will reset them so they can get right back into the game.

Variations

You can vary this game by prescribing how many things the partners can share. It can just be one thing or several.

Another variation with a large group is to have everyone walk around with their partner and introduce each other to the other pairs in a more casual way, through individual conversations.

To more strongly integrate the Nurtured Heart Approach, explicitly ask that they use experiential recognitions in their introductions:

- "Hi, this is my new friend Sue, and she likes to collect stamps. What that tells me about Sue is that she is disciplined, curious, and focused, because she has to search for all those unique stamps and keep them neatly and carefully stored."

- "Hi, this is my new friend Bob, and he has climbed five mountains. Wow! What that tells me is that he is very adventurous, courageous and probably pretty fit."

Or you can notch up this game even further and call it My Partner's Greatness. This variation can be done in a large circle. If Sue shares something unique about herself, the person on her left might say, "What that tells me about Sue's greatness is..." and so on.

Ideas for Reflection

Ask the group to call out the greatness they experienced or witnessed. "What qualities of greatness are we witnessing during the playing of this game?"

Encourage group members to give one or two recognitions based on what they observed or appreciated:

- ◉ "I am so impressed with how focused and present everyone was during the game and how much respect you showed to each other in listening to their stories."

- ◉ "How did it feel to learn something new about someone else? How did it feel to be listened to?"

- ◉ "How did you make sure you heard what your partner shared? What did you do inside or what qualities does that require?"

Connect the lesson to life:

- ◉ "Why is it important to listen to someone else's story, and to remember what they said? Why did you want to listen? Is it sometimes hard to remember what someone just shared? Why might that be? What can help you remember?"

- ◉ "What are some helpful tips in being a good listener?"

Remind students of the qualities identified at the start of the lesson. Model by recognizing students with strong appreciation and acknowledgment:

- ◉ "I am really impressed with how everyone listened and also spoke with presence and confidence... I really noticed the respect, support and focus you gave each person when they were sharing...That shows the empathy and respect you have for each other."

Support the conversation by asking what qualities they saw in others, in themselves, and in the group as a whole.

End the game and reflection time by acknowledging the group for its participation.

 Knots

Set Up
This game works best in small circles of 8 - 12 players.

If there are less than seven players per group, the problem of untying the knot is too easy; and more than 12 can be too difficult – although a large game of Knots can be wonderful if the group is up for it.

To form a knot, have everyone in the group stand shoulder to shoulder in a circle and reach his or her hands into the center.

Everybody grabs a couple of hands, making sure it is not both hands of the same person or the hand of an adjacent player.

SEL Skills

  ● Relationship skills

  ● Social awareness

  ● Cooperation

  ● Focus

  ● Problem solving

Game On

1. Ask the group to carefully untangle the knot formed by their hands and arms without breaking any connections between the hands.

2. Tell the players it is perfectly okay to readjust their grips as needed, but not to release and re-grip to solve a knot problem.

3. The group should end up as one big circle or two smaller, interlinked circles.

4. You will quickly see which group members are analysts, and which are activists. The analysts will try to figure out the problem before taking action, and the activists will dive right into it and start climbing over and under. Usually, a combination of both approaches is most helpful.

5. If the knot seems impossible, bring in the "Knot Doctor" (the teacher). Determine where the best place is to make an incision (pull apart a pair of hands and reconnect them however needed) and see if this will provide the "knot-aid" to solve the problem. Maybe 'yes'...or maybe 'knot.'

Look for Greatness

Energize:

- Accepting the challenge and reveling in the joy of solving the puzzle.

- Being cooperative and collaborative.

- Being assertive.

- Listening to other people's suggestions or instructions.

- Respecting everyone's physical comfort, abilities, and

boundaries.

- Taking the time to look at the problem carefully, having forethought, and being patient when mistakes are made.

- Kinesthetic awareness and spatial understanding.

- Working to unite body, mind, and heart through playing this game safely.

- Persistence and determination.

- Making it fun!

- Creatively using physical ability and supplementing limits with gentleness.

Clarity for Players

No breaking the knot.

No pulling or yanking of the hands you are holding.

No making suggestions disruptive of the group solving the problem.

Let the players know that you trust them to follow the rules; and that, if necessary, you will reset them so they can get right back into the game. You might recognize other qualities that support the following of rules, such as listening, offering supportive and encouraging words, or being kind to each other.

Variations

You can start the game with one or two people standing outside each circle. They are responsible for making suggestions as to how the group moves to untangle itself.

Another variation is to have one or two volunteers – the designated "untangler/s" – exit the room. Have the group hold hands in a circle and tangle themselves up into a big knot by weaving around and through one another without letting go of one another's hands. This variation can work with a much bigger group, so that 20 players can tangle themselves up and have one or two untanglers direct the group in how to untangle. This creates abundant material for positive recognitions for the untanglers!

Ideas for Reflection

Knots is the model cooperative game. It is a clear opportunity to focus on the social-emotional learning and expression of greatness that take place during cooperative play.

Help the group debrief the experience by offering simple prompts:

- "What is making this game work well?"

- "What was your favorite part of the game?"

Encourage group members to give one or two recognitions to self and/or others participating, about what they observed or appreciated:

- "I am so impressed with how cooperative everyone was during the game and how much respect you showed to each other in listening to other suggestions."

- "Is there anything you might do next time to notch it up?"

There is a real feeling of excitement when this problem is solved, so this is a great opportunity to focus on the joys of working together and solving problems:

- "How did it feel to work together with everyone?"

- "How did it feel when you successfully untangled the knot?"

Connect the game to life:

- "How do you usually solve problems? Do you see problems as something difficult to be avoided, or do you love challenges? Do you jump in and try solutions, or are you someone that analyzes a problem before you try various solutions?"

- "Do you prefer to collaborate and work with others, or are you someone who likes to work by yourself? Can you see why it is helpful to learn how to work with others? Who are people that have jobs that are all about solving problems? Engineers, doctors, software developers?"

Remind students of the qualities identified at the start of the lesson. Model recognizing students with strong appreciation and acknowledgment.

- "I am really impressed with how everyone listened to each other and offered creative solutions in a supportive manner...That shows the empathy and respect you have for each other."

Support the conversation by asking what qualities of greatness they saw in others, in themselves, and in the group as a whole. As the players learn to see the greatness in others, they will freely offer recognitions to their fellow players.

End the game and reflection time by acknowledging the group for its participation.

♥ Acknowledgements and Resets for Energizing Games

In addition to learning the skills required for playing a particular game, Nurtured Heart Play offers many opportunities to use the Nurtured Heart Approach to teach and positively acknowledge over-arching interpersonal dynamics like playing by the rules without cheating, being a good sport, being flexible and curious, and supporting fellow players. The importance of this becomes pronounced around the ages of seven to eleven, when kids love knowing and enforcing the rules. Children in this developmental stage tend to look at things as black and white, right and wrong.

The traditional role of parents, teachers, and guides has been to remind children to keep on playing fairly with others and to stay open to exploring possible solutions to problems when they arise, pointing out the choices that lead to happy outcomes, positivity, and success. From now on, all such reminders can be made in context of appreciations of fair play *while it is happening,* and in reflecting great choices that are already being demonstrated. This is the essence of Nurtured Heart Play.

If someone breaks a rule or doesn't understand a parameter of the game, it is a simple matter of stopping the action using a group reset, clarifying the rule, and starting again. Everyone understands that rules are necessary in order for a game to flow, and that you've got to know the rules to play. Knowing the rules inside and out makes possible the full-engagement flow state – that state of being totally IN the game and playing all-out. Clarifying to the group the need to follow a certain rule happens in context of appreciation once the reset is complete and the rule is no longer being broken.

If the rule is "No bumping into anyone," respond to a player bumping into another player by giving the child a reset. Stop the game if necessary to do this, but be careful not to energize the problem! Clarify the rule being broken by providing acknowledgment as soon as the child is no longer breaking the rule: "Stuart, I see you took that reset beautifully, and now you're not bumping into any other players! Great control of your body. Thanks for following that important rule that keeps everyone safe." The game flows again with everyone focused on the activity. All players have heard the reset and renewal, which means everyone got a reminder about the rule – but breaking it doesn't seem as exciting as staying in the play of the game.

This concept is so simple that kids easily understand it, and it works perfectly in the context of these group activities. Every child has learned, within play, how to reset. A reset is like the blowing of a whistle during an athletic event. Time stops. The consequence is given for the rule being broken. Then, everything returns to that starting point, without fanfare. The ball is put back in play.

Reinforce rule-following consistently throughout game play, not just following a reset. When playing Have You Ever, you could reinforce the rule of no aggressive bumping right in the process of play by saying, "Wow, I can see you are all having a lot of fun and I can see that some of you wanted to bump into each other, but didn't. That showed a lot of body awareness, cooperation, and consideration for your fellow players. Great!" Stay in a space of energizing all of the multitudes of choices being made to support the positive outcome of the game.

Energize the courage to get in the center of the circle or otherwise speak out in front of the whole group. This can be especially scary for teens, or for children who are more shy and reserved. Energize speaking clearly and loudly so that all can hear the question being asked. Energize the awareness to make other players feel comfortable, seen, and cared for through encouragement or respecting physical limits. Energize playing with delight, because it means the players love their own joy, and they are helping others to feel that joy inside themselves too. These games are great for helping groups of youth begin to get to know and trust one another, or for deepening existing connections.

In the flow, these games allow the players to open their experiences to different choices. The energetic movement and instantaneous decision-making loosens patterns of thought, brings players present in the moment, and gives the opportunity to be a chance-taker, a positive supporter, and a playful trend-setter. Watch: the least expected may jump to lead, allowing their inner guidance to shine out because they have the radiant greatness of being spontaneous.

Quick-shares around the group can be used throughout most any game. Have each student say a one-word response in relation to the last round of the game. Such shares can provide interesting pauses in the action that can be used creatively by the leader to generate and harvest more Nurtured Heart acknowledgments.

Appreciations and Recognitions: A Review

Appreciations of participants in relation to rules being followed can be smoothly interspersed along the way, relaying the beauty we see in ongoing choices to not cross the boundaries of the game. Everyone involved is invited to be fully and equally part of the game, with clear rules and infinite possibilities to try on within those boundaries.

Active Recognitions are simple, non-judgmental, incontrovertibly true descriptions of what the child/ren is/are doing. The child receiving an Active Recognition feels seen and valued. These recognitions are the kind most easily 'digested' by the resistant child who doesn't want anyone to compliment her.

"I noticed how the three of you jumped right into play ing the game after I gave instructions."

"Kim, through this entire game you have been smiling. It's nice to see you enjoying the activity."

"I know some of you wanted to be the leader and haven't gotten the chance yet. You are all still listening with all of your attention and following all of the rules!"

Experiential Recognitions add a value judgment or an acknowledgement of a specific quality of greatness to an Active Recognition.

"Callie, each gesture you did was full of expression and positive energy that exuded from your entire body. You have incredible joy and enthusiasm! The three of you were very focused and present when we started playing which I am sure contributed to your success. That took focus and concentration."

"Kay, you were so determined! I saw you get better and better at the game with each round. That kind of focus takes a keen awareness of what is going on around you."

"All of your reflections on the game have been so unique and made so many careful observations. That shows me your curiosity, creativity, and the desire to get to know your classmates."

"The way you gave that recognition to Haley with your eyes on her and a clear voice shows me how you truly care that she understands her greatness."

Proactive Recognitions are appreciations given when rules are not being broken.

"I noticed that there was no arguing during this game. You could have but you chose not to."

"Nobody rolled their eyes or complained when I gave instructions to find someone they didn't know for a partner. Instead, you found a partner and began the activity immediately."

"You all asked questions that were kind, easy to engage with, considerate of other players' feelings, and really fun! I need you all to know, that shows great thoughtfulness, intelligence, and a big desire to be friends with everyone."

"Jimmy and Kyle, I need to acknowledge both of you. I saw the looks on your faces as I was giving the instructions. You didn't look like you wanted to play this game, yet neither of you disrupted the session by yelling out, 'This is stupid!' or 'I don't want to play.' Instead, when it was time to join in, you played...and the negative looks on your faces were no longer there. In that moment, you both showed integrity and thoughtfulness."

Creative Recognitions celebrate appropriate responses to clear requests. These active games offer many opportunities to recognize the positive side of all the movements and actions and changing energies.

"Lisa and Kyle, I need both of you to find a group of three to join." And then, "You each found a group. I appreciate how quickly you chose to do that. Thank you for following my directions so beautifully."

"I need one of you to be the next leader...Caleb, you followed through with what I asked by immediately going to the middle. I appreciate your flexibility in this moment."

"I need one of you to be the next leader... Caleb and Jimmy, neither of you argued with me about what I asked. Instead, you figured out who was going to sit in the chair and who was going to be the next leader all on your own. You both showed collaboration and good judgment."

"Kim, Lisa, John and Jeffrey, I need each of you to take a few steps back...Now, we have room for everyone to be in our circle. Thanks for immediately doing what I asked without arguing or delaying."

"I need each of you to take a chair and put it against the wall for later... Paul, Jimmy, Scott, Lisa and Terry, each of you are up and moving your chairs back. You did what I asked immediately. Excellent! All of the chairs are against the wall, and everyone is back to the large group. I appreciate how each of you moved your chair so that we had the space we needed for this next activity."

"You guys immediately started the next round of the game! Your enthusiasm to keep playing with the rules I gave shows immense respect. If you felt any resistance inside, I didn't feel it at all. I feel very happy to get to play with such caring, cooperative individuals."

Where a player or players are resistant or uncooperative, Creative Recognitions can be used to 'hijack' them into complying with requests – with compliance directly followed by abundant positive recognitions. You might make a request of a child who is already in the process of doing what you are requesting, and then give that child all the credit for compliance that was in actuality kind of an accident!

Greatness Appreciations can be a choice to highlight the greatness we see, and we can acknowledge the qualities we wish to cultivate during the game.

"The group is having so much fun and everyone is really honoring each other's boundaries. This shows the greatness of respect for self and others."

"Lilly, I love how your hand shot up when I asked if anyone would like to ask the next question. You have the greatness of confidence and enthusiasm."

Resets

"Andrew, thank you for resetting so quickly by taking some deep breaths and then rejoining the game! You obviously have great confidence in your ability to immediately follow the rules again."

"Jesse, I see you reaching to support your friend with your arms. You were angry but you turned your feeling into keeping someone else safe instead. I am in awe of your beautiful dedication to being kind."

"Kaylee, reset...Kaylee, welcome back. You are now sitting in the circle without distracting your friends. You are being respectful and showing great self-control."

"Lilly, you just reset your body. You stopped your body from bumping into and touching your friends. That takes self-control and shows respect for your body and those around you. It also takes mindfulness of awareness of your body in relation to others. All of these are great qualities that I see in you."

"Jimmy, I appreciate how you noticed that everyone else had stopped talking and then you did the same. You reset yourself completely on your own, and now you are looking at me with a smile on your face. You have the greatness of self-awareness, along with unflappability and strength."

ACTIVE GAMES:

THE GREATNESS OF COOPERATION AND FUN

Active Games inspire lots of energy and positivity just by virtue of the fact that they get kids' bodies moving. This chapter includes several variations on the game of tag, some games that involve ball tossing, and one game where players get to operate their very own robots! Some games require an outdoor space or a large indoor space; others can be played in a smaller space while still being active and physically engaging. Some of these games require equipment such as soft foam balls, fleece balls, or yarn balls.

 Elbow Tag

Materials
One foam ball (optional)

Set Up
This game works for 10-20 players.

Have everyone pair off with a partner.

Partners link up by hooking their arms at the elbow joint. Explain that linked-up partners do not move in the initial playing of the game.

One pair is not joined. One person is "It" and the other is "Not-It."

You may opt to use a safe tagging item, such as a soft foam ball, for the "It" to carry and tag with.

SEL Skills

- Cooperation

- Teamwork

- Safety

Game On

1. Have the hooked-up pairs separate a few feet from each other, but not spread out too far.

2. Demonstrate how "It" runs after "Not-It" and tries to tag him or her.

3. Tagging successfully means switching roles. (No immediate tag-backs.)

4. As a Not-It is pursued, he or she can hook onto someone's elbow, joining with that person safely...which forces the other player who was hooked on to the other side to become the new Not-It.

5. This goes on until It tags someone and is replaced.

6. At any point, you can pause the game and ask the group, "What qualities of greatness are we witnessing during the playing of this game?"

Look for Greatness

Energize:

- Having fun during a challenging game.

- Taking care with one's own and others' bodies.

- Intelligently formulating a strategy.

- Enjoying the flow of playing and winning and having fun either way.

- Players working together to keep the game going, willingness to share the fun.

- Respecting physical needs (i.e. being considerate of someone who can't run as fast).

- Fluidly embracing the movements of the game, gracefully hooking arms, gliding in the space, tagging gently.

- Artful agility, enthusiasm, and playfulness.

Clarity for Players

No touching during the game in a disruptive or disrespectful manner.

No tugging or yanking on your neighbor's arm.

No arguing, roughhousing, bad words, or breaking any other of the general classroom rules while we are playing.

Let the players know that you trust them to follow the rules of the game as well as the general class rules; and that, if necessary, you will reset them so they can get right back into the game.

Variations

During the first rounds of play, the linked atoms don't move. After everyone understands how to hook and unhook, tell the pairs that they can walk around the play space.

Then add a rule that the players can unhook and hook up freely; but when unhooked, they can be tagged – so they'll need to look out!

Ideas for Reflection

Start off the appreciations by acknowledging something you saw: "I am really impressed by how everyone was aware of each other. You were graceful, agile, and gentle even though you played with vigor and enthusiasm. It really shows how mindful you were being during the game!"

Encourage group members to give one or two recognitions to self and/or others participating about what they observed or appreciated.

- "What did it take to play this game?"

- "What did each of you need to do in order for it to be fun and go smoothly?"

- "What was the evidence of those qualities?"

- "Is there anything you might do next time to notch it up?"

Inquire about participants' strategies during the playing of this game.

- "What strategies did you utilize or did you observe during the game?"

- "What was the biggest challenge?"

- "Did you receive help from other players?"

- "How did you use your body safely and respect other people's bodies?"

- "What were your favorite parts of the game and what greatness does that show?"

- "When the new rule was added – being able to let go and hook up with anyone – did that make it more fun? Was it too chaotic? Why?"

Connect the lesson to life: "Can you think of some examples in life where you have to observe and develop strategies to succeed?"

End the game and reflection-time by acknowledging the group for their exceptional participation.

 Elves and Wizards Tag

Materials

A few foam balls.

Set Up

This game works well for 15 - 40 people.

Tell participants, "In this magic kingdom, there are two creatures: wizards and elves. Wizards don't particularly like the playful, silly elves, so the wizards are always chasing the elves and trying to freeze them."

Demonstrate how a wizard touches (tags) an elf with his or her magic orb (a soft foam ball), and how the elf is frozen by the wizard's spell.

Set up boundaries with cones to create the right size playing area for the number of players. About half the size of a basketball court is good for 20-30 players.

SEL Skills

- Relationship skills

- Social awareness

- Self-management

- Self-mastery

- Confidence

Game On

1. The wizard goes to the middle of the playing area.

2. The game is started by the wizard(s) shouting, "We're going to get you, little elves; we're going to get you!"

3. All an elf can do is stand still, feet frozen to the ground, and cry out for help. An elfin cry for help involves holding one's left palm out and striking one's right fist into it rapidly, while shouting, "Help me, help me, help me..." in a high-pitched voice.

4. Fortunately, elves have their own magic. Two free elves can free a frozen elf by putting their arms around him or her, clasping their hands together, and shouting, "You are free, little elfling, you are free!"

5. Be careful, elves! If a wizard tags an elf who is trying to free another elf, he or she is frozen too.

6. Play for a few minutes or until all the elves are frozen; then, choose a new wizard and play again.

7. If there are more than 15 elves, add an extra wizard.

Look for Greatness

Energize:

- Fostering cooperation, teamwork, and helpfulness.

- Creating success by working together.

- Staying within the boundaries of the movements.

- Embracing the challenge for self-growth.

- Playing vigorously while being attentive and safe.

THE GREATNESS OF COOPERATION AND FUN

- Physical agility, especially in relation to respecting others' bodies.

- Expressing humor and joy in following the rules.

- Encouragement of other players.

Clarity for Players

No running outside of the boundaries.

No running without being aware of others.

No arguing, roughhousing, or bad words or breaking any other of the general classroom rules while we are playing.

Let the players know that you have faith they will be able to follow the rules of the game as well as the general class rules; and that, if necessary, you will reset them so they can get right back into the game.

Variations

Star Wars tag: Have "it" be from the Empire; players who are frozen adopt the posture of Han Solo frozen in carbonite. Two free rebels must put their arms around the frozen player and say, "Long live the force" to unfreeze that player.

Stuck-in-the-mud tag: When "it" tags other players, they must stand frozen with their legs stretched far apart; other players must come by and crawl through their legs to free them.

Ideas for Reflection

Encourage group members to give recognitions to self and/or others participating about what they observed or appreciated. Create momentum for this by modeling as needed:

- "Everyone played so vigorously and still played safely and maintained awareness of each other."

- "Everyone was willing to play silly roles and have fun laughing at themselves and each other kindly!"

Discuss with the group what they enjoyed, where they might notch it up, and what greatness they saw:

- "What did you enjoy about this game of tag?"

- "What did it take for you to enjoy playing together?"

- "What made it successful to stay alive and not have the whole group frozen by the 'it'?"

- "What qualities did you see in your classmates as we played?"

- "What did you see yourself doing well to help others succeed in the game?"

- "Is there any way you would notch up your teamwork with others?"

Connect the lesson to their lives:

- "When in life might you need to accept help from others?"

- "Can you remember a time when you needed help from others?"

- "How did it feel when people came to help you?"

- "Have you been in a situation where people needed your help?"

- "How did it feel to be of help to others?"

Remind students of the qualities of greatness identified at the start of the lesson. Did they see what they predicted?

Model the giving of appreciations:

- "I am really impressed how everyone followed the rules of this game and therefore kept the game really safe for everyone."

- "I also noticed all the cooperation that was going on to free all the frozen elves. It really exemplifies the teamwork and cooperative spirit you all showed that during the game!"

Support the conversation by asking what qualities they saw in others, in themselves and in the group as a whole.

End the game and reflection time by acknowledging the group for its participation.

Everybody's It Tag

Materials

Enough bandanas or small cloth 'tails' for however many players are participating (optional; see below).

Set Up

This game works well for big groups: 20-60 players.

Tell the players that this is the fastest game there is.

Everyone is "it" and everyone is compelled to try and tag others. That's it.

Demonstrate that when one player tags another, the one who has been tagged is eliminated and must sit down, squat, or put their hands on their head to indicate tagged status.

Tagging is allowed anywhere on the body aside from the spots that would always be considered "hands-off" in a public setting. Tagging the head is never allowed.

If two people tag each other at the same time, both players are out. If there is any argument about who was tagged first, both players are also automatically out.

If you aren't confident in a group's ability to tag safely with hands, play the game with players having tails (such as a sock or bandana stuck in the rear of the waistband of their pants or skirts) that must be pulled off.

Competition, Fairness, Body Awareness, and the No-Arguing Rule

This game is a great way to expend energy. It is simple and exciting. There is also the opportunity to focus on the challenge as it relates to games that have a bit of competition.

You can bring attention to the importance of body awareness by pointing out how excited we can get when playing full out. Inspire players to let the excitement and fun happen while staying in control of their bodies.

There is also a wonderful opportunity to teach emotional intelligence; to use this game as a springboard to talk about concepts of fairness. This game is great for working with cooperation in the thick of exciting play: emphasize that if two players tag each other at the same time, they can instantly agree to either both be down, or to allow one person to volunteer to be out and let the other go free rather than argue over who tagged who. You can also use the state of being "out" and being "frozen" to teach about the reset.

Being out doesn't mean you are in trouble or failing at the game – it is just a moment to regroup and prepare to re-enter the fun of the game.

Always enforce the rule about arguing. Any argument about who is out means that both players involved in that argument are automatically out.

SEL Skills

- Relationship skills

- Social awareness

- Self-management

- Body awareness

- Respectful choices

Game On

1. The group spreads out within a marked-off area. At the signal to start the game, each person attempts to tag someone else.

2. This fast action continues until only one player remains.

3. If there are only a few players left, have them move toward each other and attempt to tag each other. Then, just as the victor begins to congratulate him or herself, shout, "Everyone is free, let's play again. Ready 1, 2, 3, go!"

4. The action begins anew.

Look for Greatness

Energize:

- Awareness of the group and of moving safely in the space.

- Enjoying the excitement and fast pace of the game.

- Mastery of having a relaxed mind and being present amongst seeming chaos.

- Agility and bodily control.

- Acceptance of being tagged out and coming back to the game renewed.

- Honoring and being sensitive to other's levels of ability and helping the game be fun for everyone.

- Amazing effort and fully engaging one's own abilities (and enjoying it!).

- Cooperation and fairness to create community amongst competition.

- Gentle tagging.

Clarity for Players

No tagging in a hard or hurtful way.

No arguing about being tagged.

No bad words or not following the other usual rules of the group.

Let the players know that you have faith they will be able to follow the rules of the game as well as the general class rules; and that, if necessary, you will reset them so they can get right back into the game.

Variations

Hospital Tag: Each player gets a Band-aid (a free hand) to place on the spot that has just been tagged, then the next hand. Only after the third tag are they fully frozen. This is a good one to try after a few rounds of Elbow Tag.

Perpetual Tag: When the player that tagged you is tagged, you are back up and free.

Ideas for Reflection

Encourage group members to give one or two recognitions to self and/or others participating about what they observed or appreciated. Create momentum for this by modeling as needed: "I am so impressed with how fairly everyone played and how much fun everyone was having."

Ask the group:

- "What challenges did you encounter during the game?"

- "What surprised you about your fellow players?"

- "What were your favorite parts of the game?"

- "Even though everyone was playing individually, what did we do to make this game fun for all? What does it take to do those things? Are there other situations that you have to do the same or similar things in order for everyone to enjoy themselves?"

Tag is a favorite of children everywhere. Explore the reasons for this:

- "Why is it fun to chase others and to be chased?"

- "Where else in life do we like thrills? Amusement parks, scary movies..."

Connect the lesson to their lives:

- "Does it feel exciting to challenge yourself physically?

- "What are some fun ways in life that people challenge themselves?"

- "Why is this a good kind of thrill, where as others are not as good for us?"

This game also has the moment of choosing fairness and settling arguments when simultaneous tags appear to happen:

- "Do we sometimes argue because we think we are right?"

- "What qualities does it take for us to let someone else have their opinion and let go of our own opinion or observation?"

Remind students of the qualities identified at the start of the lesson. Did they see what they predicted? Model by recognizing students with strong appreciation and acknowledgment: "I am really impressed how everyone followed the very specific rules of this game and stayed in control of their bodies and therefore kept the game really safe for everyone. It really shows how caring and respectful you were being!" Support the conversation by asking what qualities they saw in others, in themselves and in the group as a whole.

End the game and reflection time by acknowledging the group for its participation.

Hug Tag

Materials

A soft foam ball.

Set Up

This game works well for 15 - 40 players.

Demonstrate to the players that a hug can be anything from an arm around another player's shoulders to a full hug.

Give one or two players a soft ball or other object with which to tag. This object indicates that player is "It."

Designate one player per 15 players as "It."

Set up boundaries. The game works best in an area that's not too large. Half the size of a basketball court would work well for 20-30 players.

Teaching Body Intelligence Through Play

It takes focus, awareness, and readiness to play this game with kindness and safe touch. It is important to set clear parameters for the playing of the game. Use this game as a springboard to talk about personal boundaries around touch. Setting and respecting these boundaries, and being really clear with rule following, is a vital component in the Nurtured Heart Approach. Hug Tag is all about playing safely and respecting other people's physical boundaries.

For example, let's say Sue didn't want to be hugged, and said so at the start of the game. "Sue said no hugs, and then said she didn't want your arm on her shoulder...

so you offered her your arm to just hold and she took it. You were being very respectful of her body and her decision about what was comfortable and not comfortable, and you were able to do this in a fast-paced game."

Before playing this game, be sure your group is ready for this level of touch. Ask the players to let each other know what will make this game safe for them. As in many traditional tag games, there is a "safe place," a home base where you are safe from being tagged. In this game the home base is being hugged. What fun!

SEL Skills

- Relationship skills
- Social awareness
- Self-regulation
- Social norms
- Respectful choices

Game On

1. Players who are "It" try to tag other players. When a player is tagged, he or she becomes "It" and is given the tagging item. No tag-backs.

2. If players are hugging someone, they are safe.

3. If everyone is hugging someone, the game grinds to a halt. So the final rule is: an "It" can go up to two players who are hugging and count loudly to five. These two players must split up by the count of five.

Look for Greatness

Energize:

- Balancing competition with being gentle and kind with players' bodies.

- Showing playfulness, respectfulness, or even affection with touch.

- Participants being clear and honest about their boundaries, indicating self-knowledge.

- Successful non-verbal communication to work out physical limits with others.

- Willingness to challenge one's comfort zone.

- Using the boundaries to experience full-on play.

- Expressing and spreading joy through contact.

- Gracefully moving in the game.

- Fast and safe responses to situations.

Clarity for Players

No grabbing roughly or being physically too aggressive when hugging.

No running in an unsafe manner, with inadequate awareness of others.

No arguing, roughhousing, bad words, or breaking any other of the general classroom rules while playing.

Let the players know that you trust them to follow the rules of the game as well as the general class rules; and that, if necessary, you will reset them so they can get right back into the game.

Variations

Change the number of people who have to be hugging to be safe: try groups of three, four, or even seven!

Try starting the game with players in groups of two or three, hugging already. Give a signal to switch groups; in the scramble, "It" will probably find someone to tag. Call out to switch again.

Ideas for Reflection

Encourage group members to give recognitions to self and/or others participating about what they observed or appreciated. Then add, "Is there anything you might do next time to notch it up, to make the game work better and be more fun for everyone?"

This game involves lots of playful touching. It takes focus, awareness, and readiness to play safely. Asking the group about their experience will help them to focus on and reflect upon each other's greatness in making the game work well, which is useful if any discomfort arises:

- "What did you or another player do to help everyone to have fun playing this game?"

- "What did you appreciate about someone else while playing this game?"

Connect the lesson to life:

- "Have you had times in life where people try to hug you without asking for permission? How did that feel?"

- "In this game we are giving each other permission to hug us. In life, how can we set boundaries we need for hugging or touch?"

- "What does it take to set our own boundaries and honor those of others? What are some examples of your successes in doing that, today or at other times?"

End the game and reflection time by acknowledging the group for its exceptional participation.

Group Juggle

Materials

A number of soft tossing balls.

Set Up

This game works well for 8 - 20 players.

Have the group form a circle. One person will be the designated starter. The starter has a number of soft tossing balls.

It's fun to ask how many people in the group can juggle. Say, "That's great. And it's okay if you don't, because now, we are all going to learn how to juggle as a group."

SEL Skills

- Relationship skills

- Social awareness

- Managing stress

- Cooperation

- Teamwork

- Focus

- Self-regulation

- Optimism

Game On

1. The starter starts by tossing a ball to a particular person across the circle. This first person will throw to that same person every time.

2. This second person raises his hand to indicate he has already received it and then tosses the ball across the circle to a new person.

3. This continues until everyone has a hand up, indicating each person has caught the ball once.

4. The pattern completes by coming back to the person who started it.

5. Repeat the pattern to make sure everyone knows it, and then commence to send the ball around as quickly as possible.

6. Begin adding more balls. If people drop the balls, just get the balls going again.

Look for Greatness

Energize:

- Being alert and responsive.

- Paying attention and focusing on one task at a time.

- Finding humor and lightheartedness in mistakes.

- Staying keen and relaxed in the midst of chaos.

- Using breathing to stay present, even when excited.

- Having a sharp mind for multi-tasking.

- Great self-regulation in an activity of anticipation.

- Having fun with a challenge.

- Contributing to cooperation around the success of the group.

- Kinesthetic awareness and physical abilities when throwing or moving in the space.

Clarity for Players

No purposely tossing the ball too fast or making it too difficult to catch.

No disrupting your teammates in the circle from getting ready to catch the ball.

No arguing, roughhousing, bad words, or breaking any other of the general classroom rules while playing.

Let the players know that you trust them to follow the rules of the game as well as the general class rules; and that, if necessary, you will reset them so they can get right back into the game.

Variations

Try adding a command: toss in slow motion, or at hyper-speed.

Try reversing the throwing pattern.

Another variation is called "busy streets." Once a pattern has been established have the leader, who is holding 4-5 balls, walk across and hand the ball to the next person in the correct sequence and take their place in the circle. Now that person does the same, walking across and handing this ball to their person in that set order. After the ball has been passed to a couple more people, the leader starts another ball, thus essentially juggling people with the ball being the indicator for the exchange point. The leader continues in this pattern, starting a few more balls. After a couple of times through, the leader stops and allows the balls to finish with them, at the starting point.

With younger children, have them sit and roll the balls across the circle to create the pattern. The balls often collide, bringing out lots of laughter.

Ideas for Reflection

Encourage group members to give one or two recognitions to self and/or others participating about what they observed or appreciated. Then add, "What was going well that you or others did, and how do you think you can notch the game up next time?"

This game plays with breaking a complex activity into its basic steps. It involves doing your collaborative part to create the group experience. It takes focus, concentration, and patience to create the pattern. Ask participants:

- "How did it feel to try something that seemed to be very difficult?"

- "Did you have greater and greater success after more practice? If so, why?"

- "What made it easier to do?"

- "Do you think we may have been able to do it faster? How would we have done that?"

Connect the lesson to life:

- "Where are there times when we are juggling, doing a number of things at once? Does it help to focus on just one thing at a time?"

In this game there will certainly be dropped balls and other mistakes.

- "What happens when we make mistakes? Do we jump right back in and try again, or do we stop and analyze why we made the mistake? Do we ask for ideas on how to do it better?"

- "What attitude about mistakes will be most helpful?"

- "Do we ask for help when this gets really challenging? Can you think of instances in everyday life where you need to ask for help?"

- "What great qualities does it take to ask for help? Openness, curiosity, flexibility, acceptance...?"

- "What are some examples of your successes in doing that, asking for help, today or at other times?"Support the conversation by asking what qualities they saw in others, in themselves, and in the group as a whole.

End the game and reflection time by acknowledging the group for their exceptional participation.

Robots of Greatness

Set Up
This game works well for 20 - 60 people.

Find a large enough open space to accommodate people moving freely, although a few obstacles can be incorporated into the game.

Ask for two volunteers to come up and demonstrate the game.

Tell a story of how the great scientist, the robot master, has created these amazing robots of greatness. They have great agility and will always communicate when they are in danger.

Demonstrate how each robot is controlled by three different commands. A tap on the right shoulder turns the robot in a 90-degree angle turn to the right. A tap on the left shoulder turns the robot 90 degrees to the left, and a tap on both shoulders at the same time turns the robot 180 degrees around. The robots may only go in a straight line until the robot master changes their direction.

If a robot should run into an obstacle, like another robot, it stops just short of bumping into that obstacle and sends out its danger signal, such as "beep-beep-beep," until the robot master redirects the troubled android.

SEL Skills

- Relationship skills

- Social awareness

- Self-management

- Self-mastery; confidence

- Cooperation

Game On

1. Have groups of three decide who is the first robot master and who are the two robots.

2. "Robot masters, you have made these amazing robots of greatness. Their greatness is that they move in very precise, straight lines. They never deviate from moving in a straight line. How great is that? Another part of their greatness is that they have a proximity detector, so they always stop one foot away from any obstacle and make their own unique danger signal so their master can come and redirect them."

3. Have each group determine its own unique robot locomotion and danger signals: for example, "chuck-chuck-chuck-chuck" for locomotion and "beep-beep-beep" for danger. It

can be any noise! "Ping," "Glug," "Boing," and "Swish" are other examples. Give groups a chance to demonstrate their signals before play begins.

4. One person must act as the human robot master who starts up and guides his or her robots.

5. "Okay, robot masters, there is a switch on the back of your robot — that's how you turn it on and off. Ready? Turn your robots on!"

6. Each robot master turns his or her robots on, and the game is in full swing!

7. Once you feel all the teams have had a chance to fully dive in, command everyone to stop. Have the robot masters collect their robots.

8. Players switch roles.

9. Play at least two more times so each player gets to be a robot master.

Look for Greatness
Energize:

- Players who may not normally take leadership embracing being the robot controller.

- Robots following guidance from their controller with responsiveness and ease.

- Acceptance of direction from peers.

- Using bodily control to respect physical boundaries of others.

- Restraint in staying within the boundaries of the game rules.

- Playfulness and humor in a wacky situation!

- Being fully in character as the robot.

- Inventive movements and noises.

- Trusting the sense of belonging as part of the group.

- Creating emotional safety for other players by encouraging their creativity and exuberance!

- Frolicking in the physical energy of the movements.

Clarity for Players

No bumping, pushing, or contacting any other robot.

No changing directions on your own. You must wait for the robot master to direct you.

No arguing, roughhousing, or bad words or breaking any other of the general classroom rules while playing.

Let the players know that you have faith they will be able to follow the rules of the game as well as the general class rules; and, if necessary, you will reset them so they can get right back into the game.

Variations

Let each individual robot make its own locomotion and danger sounds.

Each robot invents its particular repetitive movements in addition to the noise signals. A robot might shuffle, slide, or lunge along in a straight line!

With younger children, just have one robot per robot controller.

For families, it can be great to have the child be the robot master and the parent be the robot.

Do you dare to try this with three robots and one robot controller?

Ideas for Reflection

Encourage group members to give one or two recognitions to self and/or others participating about what they observed or appreciated. Remind students of the qualities identified at the start of the lesson. Did they see what they predicted? Model by recognizing students with strong appreciation and acknowledgment. Examples: "I am really impressed how everyone followed the very specific rules of this game and therefore kept the game really safe for everyone. It really shows how caring and respectful you were being during play!"

Ask the group for creative ideas for new ways to direct the robots or to change the game to add variety. Be sure to provide appreciations for willingness to brainstorm.

Discuss game play:

- "What challenge did you encounter during the game?"
- "What surprised you about your fellow players?"
- "What were your favorite parts of the game?"
- "Was it easy or hard to follow the very specific directions of this game?"
- "Which role, the robot or the director, did you like better and why?"
- "Why do these two [robot and robot master] need each other to make the game work?"

Connect the lesson to their lives:

- "How does it feel to be the robot master, the one that is powerful and in control?"

- "How did it feel to be the robot, having to follow the directional control of the robot master?"

- "Can you remember a time when you didn't feel in control?"

- "How does it feel when a leader gives direction in a kind and thoughtful way?"

- "How does it feel if a leader gives commands in an unfriendly and demanding way?"

- "Can you think of an example where someone is the master and you have to follow their commands?"

End the game and reflection time by acknowledging the group for its participation.

Acknowledgements and Resets for Active Games

A few years ago, a school district in Massachusetts banned the game of tag. Their rationale: tagging can be too aggressive; children get hurt; children who are not as fast as the others may feel shame. The adults that made this decision probably had good intentions in responding to children's upsets and hurts; however, it was an overreaction. The game itself was blamed for problems that are easily handled through appropriate supervision and guidance.

It is enormously important for children to get enough movement throughout the day. For younger children, this often takes the form of chasing and fleeing. This is a primary impulse in all animals—partly as training for predator and prey skills. Deer do it; squirrels do it; cats and dogs do it; dolphins do it, and certainly, children love to do it. The key here is to be sure that players understand the rules around being safe with each other, and consistently expressing gratitude when everything is going along safely and smoothly – when unsafe behaviors are *not* happening. The stronger the focus on the positive results of playing with good form, the less likely the opposite will occur.

Tag games present really great opportunities for reset practice. Kids will often argue over whether they've been tagged or not: "I got you!" "No, you didn't—I got you first!" When introducing tag games, demonstrate that if this happens, if there is an argument about who got whom first, both players are tagged out. If, in that moment where both players feel the tag was simultaneous, they can immediately negotiate it and one person volunteers to be tagged out – or they both agree to reset – they have managed it on their own successfully. Your role, then, is to celebrate their successful resets, where they were willing to let go of being right and move on to the next moments of being in the flow of the game. This is another example of the way in which Nurtured Heart Play creates opportunities to practice self-regulation, conflict resolution, and resetting the emotional state, all while prioritizing the child's needs for acknowledgment, engagement, and creative expression and sense of feeling connected, included, and safe.

Remember to use NHA recognitions to energize as many facets of success as possible, focusing on effort, commitment, emotional management, and cooperative play:

"Wow, I saw you really cooperating with your friends."

"Joe, I saw that you were a little frustrated when you got tagged, and then you took a moment to reset and got back in the game with enthusiasm."

"Suzie, I noticed that you saw Tim was frozen for a little while, and you went over and freed him."

Here are a few additional examples of each kind of Nurtured Heart recognition:

Active Recognitions help participants feel seen for positive details of their basic participation.

- "Laney, you waited and gave Jacob a few moments to get started before you started chasing him."

- "We now have three people being chased and you are all running and chasing without running into anyone."

- "Jacob, I noticed how gently you touched those you tagged out."

- "Kim, you were the first one tagged out and you immediately went over, sat down and waited while the game continued."

- "Sue, you told Haley exactly what was ok and not ok

for you, and you said it very clearly."

- "I noticed you really using your voice and movements to get into your role in the game."

Experiential Recognitions point out qualities of greatness. They can beautifully combine with Active Recognitions to provide detailed evidence of qualities of greatness and positive values in the person being acknowledged:

- "Sam, you are so determined to obey the rules of the game. You are modeling the way you enjoy playing for everyone; respectfully and with awareness."

- "Thank you, Robin, for your incredible choice to be kind just then. I could see you struggling in your body to remain calm, even though it looked like you were angry. I admire your decision because you trusted your inner strength."

- "You did not move until you were unfrozen; that shows great mental and physical strength."

- "The more times we played, the more you all strategized to keep the game going longer to help each other to stay in the game. That is amazing collaboration!"

- "Lisa, you kept watching who you could help in the game, and always took the chance to do so. I admire your big heart for wanting others to be successful and having fun too."

- "You lowered your voice just as I was asking you to,

Jacob. I see you paying attention to how you can best be part of the play and your determination to adjust your actions accordingly."

- "You were paying attention, which takes focus and anticipation. All the while, you were showing great enthusiasm for the game."

- "Haley, you chose to play the game with us. You could have chosen not to, but your decision to play shows that deep down, you really wanted to try something that looked fun. I applaud how in touch you are with your emotions and your bravery to do what you want."

Proactive Recognitions teach the rules by giving positive appreciation to children when they are following the rules. Greatness recognitions can be added on to deepen the experience for the participant:

- "When you were the one to tag others, you did not throw the ball; you gently tagged them on the arm or back. You have the greatness of respect, safety, gentleness, and consideration."

- "Jacob and Henry, when the two of you ended up being hooked up, neither of you appeared to be angry with the other. You didn't tug or yank the other's arm; you didn't say rude things; and when you were tagged, it didn't end up in a fight. You both know how to do all of these things. You chose not to, though. I also know the two of you have been really working on getting along

THE GREATNESS OF COOPERATION AND FUN

better, and today you both showed your determination and your intention in doing this. In both of you I see the greatness of restraint, respect, and integrity."

Creative Recognitions celebrate desired responses to clear requests. The facilitator can instigate the success of following requests by making them very simple and spotting what the participant is likely to succeed at anyway:

- "Alice, you looked around to see what the other players are doing. I see you wanting to be in the flow of the game and following the rules."

- "Josh, you are walking toward your team members; thank you for getting ready to start the game!"

- "Kyle, Lisa and Rebecca, I need you all to take four steps back...Rebecca, you did exactly as I asked. Thank you. Kyle and Lisa, I see that you two have also spread out, as I had asked you to. I appreciate your willingness to move so quickly. That takes selflessness and consideration for the group."

- "I need everyone to come over to this side of the room for instructions...I want to recognize all of you for moving to this side of the room when I asked. Many of you were talking with friends and still did as I asked. All of you were being respectful and considerate of the group."

CHAPTER FIVE ♥ ACTIVE GAMES

Resets for Active Games

"I need everyone to stop talking...No one is talking now. You have all reset your voices."

"Rodney, reset."..."Welcome back! That was fast! Let's play."

"Jacob just ran into you and I saw you start to react, and then you stopped yourself. You reset your body! You have the greatness of self-control and determination."

"Reset, Jimmy."..."Jimmy, you are no longer talking. I appreciate you resetting your voice. You are showing your integrity and respect to the group."

"Sara, reset."..."You are no longer being rough with the other elves. You are now being safe and considerate of others' bodies. You willingly made the choice to reset your body. Thank you."

"Tim, reset."..."Tim, you reset your body and are now being safe as you run around tagging others. That takes self-control and good decision making."

CHAPTER SIX

IMPROV
THEATER GAMES:
THE GREATNESS OF RISK-TAKING, CREATIVITY, AND FOLLOWING RULES

This chapter on Improv Theater Games contains just a small sampling of games in this vast category. These activities are great fun, especially with groups that have gotten to know one another and feel relatively safe to take risks and play big. They provide opportunities for players to move just to the edge of or beyond their comfort zones around public speaking and/or performing. Don't be surprised if you find several latent actors or comedians in your group while playing these games...and be prepared for a lot of laughter. Searching the Web for Improv Games will yield many, many more fun options for improvisational play.

Below, find a few guidelines that will enhance all players' experience of these games:

Improvisational Theater Guidelines

"*Yes, And...*" This important improvisational theater concept entails saying "yes" to whatever has been created, and to work with and build upon that. For example: "*Yes*, the rhinoceroses got into the purple paint, *and* when they got in the water to wash it off, all the frogs turned purple too."

Ask players to work intentionally with this concept in any improv game you lead.

Dare to be average. In improv games, the most basic of actions can be the most fun. Sometimes when people try too hard to be funny, they aren't! Keeping it simple can actually yield the most entertaining results. For example: when asked the question, "What are you doing?" and the response is "washing the dog," there is lots of room for creativity in acting out such a simple action. A response of, "I am riding my really cool motorcycle on Mars, chasing after the aliens who kidnapped my sister" might be fascinating – but is very hard to act out.

In the Nurtured Heart Approach, we see the everyday beauty of others' characters and the uniqueness that they express continually, even in the simplest of everyday actions. "Wow, you were so kind and supportive of your friend. I notice that you take the time to be caring with your friends each and every day." An expression like this can be generated about the most mundane actions. This is what makes this approach so powerful. We don't have to do anything extraordinary or highly accomplished to be recognized. The simple presence and basic participation of students are loaded with beautiful aspects of greatness that are cause for celebration.

Make your partner look good. This is all about being supportive of your partner's experience. For example, in the game "What Are You Doing?," the response to the question, "What are you doing?" could be, "I am picking my nose." Improv rules dictate saying "yes" to whatever comes our way, so players have an opportunity to be considerate of the comfort of others. Energize players who give their partners tasks that they can jump into eagerly, without embarrassment. "One of the things we talked about before playing this game was the importance of making your partner look good, and you did that beautifully. You put your partner first, which ended up being a win-win situation for both of you. You have the greatness of personal power and selflessness."

 Human Machine

Set Up

This activity works well with 6-30 people.

The group sits or stands in a large circle or audience style.

Explain that everyone is going to build a machine, collectively, by adding one person at a time.

Demonstrate with two or three volunteers.

Initially, it may be best to state that parts of the machine should not touch. Later, add that they may contact others, but may not lean on them.

SEL Skills

- Relationship skills

- Social awareness

- Body awareness

- Creativity

Game On

1. One player starts the game by stepping into the center and doing a repetitive movement and a corresponding sound.

2. Another player joins in, adding another movement and sound.

3. One by one, players join the machine, becoming its cogs and gears.

4. After all players have joined, the machine's movements speed up and the sounds grow louder.

5. To end the game, have players slow the machine down until it comes to a complete stop.

Look for Greatness

Energize:

- Creative contributions and collaborations with movements and sounds.

- Respectfulness of players' own and others' bodies.

- Playfulness and persistence with the process of the game.

- Bravery for joining in the play or being silly.

- Being present to the joy and whimsy of group creativity.

- Attentiveness to the rules.

- Flowing and showing flexibility.

Clarity for Players

No touching that disrupts another's movements.

No criticisms of anyone's creative choices.

No jumping up and joining without being chosen by the leader.

Any other regular rules of relationship, such as: no bad words, no name-calling, no disrespect, no arguing.

Let players know that you trust them to follow the rules of the game as well as the general class rules; and that, if necessary, you will reset them so they can get right back into the game.

Variations

Have students brainstorm what the next machine makes. Perhaps this one makes balloons, bubblegum, or a star; or even qualities of greatness like kindness, enthusiasm, or joy.

Try having players speed up the machine's activity until it collapses from over-exertion.

Ideas for Reflection

Take time to sit with players afterwards and remind them of the qualities identified before the game. Ask questions to assist in reflection and appreciation of self and group:

- What kind of machines could be built in the future?

- What did players notice about each person's unique movement and sound choices?

- What were players' favorite parts of the game?

- What are examples of the creative process that exist in life? (Examples: being in a band or a play; being on an engineering team designing cars.)

- How does it feel to be part of collaboration, making something unique, or supporting other people's creativity?

- Ask players for their ideas about how to make this game

more fun or rewarding in future iterations.

Memory Loss (Fill in the Blank)

Set Up

This activity works well for anywhere from two to 30 people.

Set up a chair for each person. (Participants may also sit on the floor.)

Space paired players together throughout the room so that partners can easily hear each other.

Players sit facing their partners.

One person will start as the main storyteller, with the other person being the support who fills in the blank.

Decide who will play which role first.

Have the whole group suggest a topic for the first story, such as going on vacation or going grocery shopping.

SEL Skills

- Social awareness
- Listening
- Creativity and spontaneity
- Teamwork

Game On

1. Demonstrate with a volunteer.

2. The first player begins telling a real or invented story, but then has a "memory loss" after about one or two sentences, indicated by fumbling and not having any words

except, "Um, uh, hmm..."

3. The other player then "fills in the blank" by giving the storyteller a word or phrase. The storytelling player takes this idea and continues the story, incorporating this new idea.

4. Have players continue for about two minutes with the storytelling, including numerous memory losses to allow the creation of a collaborative story between the two players.

5. Ask players to try to bring their story to a resolved ending in the next 20 seconds.

6. After the first round, explain the concept of "Yes, and..." (See below.)

7. Switch roles, pick a new subject, and do it again.

Look for Greatness
Energize:

- Partners listening attentively.

- Use of the "Yes, and..." structure to collaborate and build a story together.

- Constructive and inventive contributions to the story.

- Willingness to speak and be creative in front of others; willingness to be vulnerable.

- Sharing control of the story with partner.

- Accepting the way the narrative changes and develops.

- Positive encouragement between partners.

- Expressing creativity and the greatness of imagination.

Clarity for Players

No making suggestions that would be uncomfortable for one's partner.

No talking too loudly so as to disturb the other players during the game.

No side talking or distracting self or others when instructions are being given.

No interrupting the storyteller unless prompted by the "memory loss."

Let the players know that you trust them to follow the rules of the game as well as the general class rules; and that, if necessary, you will reset them so they can get right back into the game.

Variations

The facilitator creates story ideas for the group to allow focus on particular themes.

Play in groups of three; one person tells the story and the other two players alternate filling in the blank.

One person can stand in front of the entire group to tell the story while other players raise their hands to fill in the blank.

Ideas for Reflection

Give partners time to give one or two recognitions to self and partner. Also do this once the group has gathered together as a whole for reflection time. Model this by appreciating a few of the players yourself. This is a great time to acknowledge individuals in the group for their participation, focus, enthusiasm, patience, and listening and speaking skills.

Ask the group what they liked about the game and to brainstorm more ideas for future storytelling.

Ask the group for its observations about the game; what qualities are required of players? (Vulnerability, listening, creativity, imagination, patience, silliness...)

Bring players toward acknowledging the greatness of these qualities in the other players:

- "What surprised you about your fellow players?"

- "What did it take for your partner to listen the whole time to your story?"

- "What qualities of greatness did your partner show when making up a good story?"

How does this game connect with the rest of their lives? Ask them to think about listening and sharing.

- "How does it affect you when your peers listen very attentively to you when you are speaking?"

- "How does it feel to hear something that is really meaningful to another person?"

Talk about the "Yes, and..." structure, ask how players witness it or could apply it in everyday life.

- "How does it feel to work with someone else's imagination?"

- "How did it feel to respond with 'Yes' instead of 'No'? Did you listen or think differently?"

- "How does learning to say yes to things and be positive help with life's challenges?"

End by creatively acknowledging the group for its effort and participation: "Thank you for taking the time to see your own and each other's greatness; for playing joyfully with each other; for being respectful; for making funny and entertaining stories; and for seriously thinking about what the game shows us."

♥ Human Statue

Set Up

This game works well with 10-30 people.

Start with everyone in a large circle or seated audience-style, leaving lots of space for the activity.

Explain that the group is going to build a collective statue by each person adding to it, one at a time.

Bring up two or three participants to give an initial demonstration, coaching them through it.

Tell the group that it is okay to touch another person, but not to put their full weight on someone else's body. Demonstrate what it looks like to be in contact without anyone having to support anyone else's weight in any way.

SEL Skills

- Relationship skills
- Social awareness
- Body awareness
- Creativity
- Focus
- Self-regulation

Game On

1. One player starts the game by going into the center, creating a pose that he or she can hold for at least a minute.

2. Another person joins in, choosing something that works with, complements, or adds to this growing statue.

3. Each person can choose to be in contact or not in contact with the other players in the statue.

4. More players join in until the leader or the group feels that it's done.

5. Ask for suggestions in the naming of the statue.

6. The players then leave one at a time, in the same order they went in; the last person that went in stays and holds that pose.

7. A new statue is built starting with this last person's pose.

8. Ask the players to notice how this Human Statue changes as each person leaves. Remind the players that this game requires focus, stillness, and close observation as the statue changes forms.

Look for Greatness

Energize:

- Awareness, care, and respect of self and others' space, body, and needs.

- Helping to maintain physical safety.

- Cooperating with others to create a relational experience, creatively utilizing time and space.

- Presence to the transience of the statue; responding to the flowing nature of making art.

- Developing kinetic sensitivity, stillness-discipline, and physical agility.

- Creatively trying to convey an idea, feeling, or quality through the statue.

- Willingness to share close space and connection with others.

- Mindful collaboration and support for others' creativity and bridging ideas.

- Patience in the changing pace of the process.

Clarity for Players

No leaning on someone else such that they are supporting your weight.

No criticisms of anyone's creative choices.

No jumping up and joining without being chosen by the leader.

Let the players know that you trust them to follow the rules of the game as well as the general class rules; and that, if necessary, you will reset them so they can get right back into the game.

Variations

This is a great activity to use to depict a scenario from classroom curriculum. "Let's build a statue that represents..." the story we just read; the Transcontinental Railroad; the classical piece of music we listened to.

Build a statue at the end of class to reflect the qualities of greatness the group saw expressed during the day: kindness, playfulness, studiousness, joy. "Let's build a statue that represents self-control!"

Break the group into smaller groups and secretly give them prompts or let players come up with their own situations: have participants build a bicycle, or depict people shopping for groceries or a family having breakfast. Then, have the group display its statue while the other groups guess what it is depicting.

After the group has played a few times, the leader may be able to relax the rule about choosing the order of participants joining the statue; from that point forward, allow players to join when they feel moved to by the creative process.

Ideas for Reflection

Encourage group members to give one or two recognitions to self and/or others about what they observed or appreciated. Set the example with a recognition of your own: "I am so impressed by how collaborative and creative our class was. I really enjoyed the feeling of forming something together that was unique and fun to watch."

Ask the group for creative ideas for future statues they could build. Be sure to provide appreciations for this brainstorming of ideas.

Ask the group questions to generate reflection on the process :

- What did you notice about each person's ability to keep his or her body still and balanced?"

- "What made it easy and possible in this game to maintain mindfulness and flow?"

- "What creativity or inventiveness did you see in people's choices about how to add on to the statue?"

- "What were your favorite parts of the game?"

Connect the lesson to their lives:

- "Where in life is it helpful to be able to focus and be still and balanced in your body or mind?"

- "How does it feel to be part of a group making a project like this? How does it feel to support other people's creativity?"

- "Could you relate the qualities needed by this game to a profession...for example, being part of a dance company, or a surgeon with steady hands, or an observant scientist?""

Remind the players of the qualities of greatness identified before the game and model by giving strong appreciation and acknowledgment. "I am really impressed with the creative and considerate ways you joined the statue. I noticed the thoughtfulness, cleverness and expressiveness in people's choices as they joined the ever-changing statue." Support the conversation by asking what qualities they saw in others, in themselves and in the group as a whole.

End the game and reflection time by acknowledging group members for their participation.

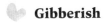 **Gibberish**

Set Up
This game works well with 3-30+ people.

First, have everyone try babbling and making strange, unusual and nonsensical gibberish sounds for about ten seconds so everyone gets silly together.

Divide the group into pairs. Demonstrate how it sounds to speak in a brand new language—a language of gibberish.

Pick an everyday subject: the weather, what they had for breakfast, or what they are going to do when they get home from school. Participants converse in pairs about the chosen topic in gibberish for about thirty seconds, for practice.

Then, create new groupings of three for the more advanced version of Gibberish Translator, described below in the "Game On" section.

SEL Skills

- Relationship skills

- Listening

- Creativity

- Spontaneity

- Teamwork

Game On

1. Divide the group into subgroups of three.

2. Demonstrate that the two people speaking gibberish each have their own made-up language and cannot understand each other. They need a translator.

3. One person acts as the translator. One of the speakers begins with a statement in gibberish; the translator translates this statement so that the other speaker can understand. Now the second speaker responds to the statement in their gibberish language and the translator relays this to the first speaker. This goes back and forth.

4. Have the translator introduce a problem that gets solved, which makes the conversation dynamic and fun.

5. End with the players in their groups of three sharing with each other what greatness they witnessed during the game.

Look for Greatness

Energize:

- Silliness, playfulness, joy, humor—qualities that require being comfortable in individuality!

- Imagination, creativity and spontaneity.

- Willingness to let feelings of awkwardness and embarrassment transform into playfulness and delight.

- Wonder-filled exploration of the variety of dialects that can be created.

- Expressiveness, enthusiasm, or eloquence when speaking.

- Mental flexibility and verbal dexterity when improvising speech on the spot.

- Embracing the safety of the situation to let imagination shine.

- Supportive listening and contributing appropriately to the conversation, as well as sharing airtime with partner or group.

Clarity for Players

Remind the gibberish players to wait for the translator to translate before responding.

No making translations that would make your partners feel uncomfortable.

No talking loudly enough to disturb the other players during play.

No negative judgments about people's creative choices.

No side talking or distractions when instructions are being given.

Let the players know that you trust them to follow the rules of the game as well as the general class rules; and that, if necessary, you will reset them so they can get right back into the game.

Ideas for Reflection

Ask the group what successes did they see during the game, in their partner or in themselves? What qualities did it take to have these successes?

Encourage group members to give one or two recognitions to self and/or others. Create momentum for this by modeling as needed.

This game lends itself to many deeper reflections:

- "Did this game feel silly to you? How does it feel to be silly? Did anyone feel embarrassed or otherwise held back when they were being silly? If so, why?"

- "Did this game create lots of laughter? Is laughter good for you?"

Connect the lesson to their lives:

- "How does it affect you when you are too self-conscious or restrained to do something?"

- "Do people sometimes say silliness is childish and you have to grow out of it? When is it okay to be silly and when is it time to be serious and how do you know the difference?"

- "When might there be a time where silliness is a good thing or where being lighthearted helps? For example: when a friend is feeling down or a child is feeling upset and you want to cheer them up, or when you have made a mistake and are being hard on yourself?"

Discuss communication:

- ◉ "Did you notice that even though you couldn't understand the gibberish, you could still understand what someone was trying to say? What made that possible? Seeing someone's body language or emotionality, or hearing the tone of their voice?"

- ◉ "How do you think we create languages? What do you think underlays all the different languages of the world? Emotions, needs, ideas?"

Go back to the qualities of greatness identified before the game, and ask players to reflect upon whether they found those qualities in themselves or in others. "Did you learn how to create spontaneously in the moment and was it fun being silly and laughing together?" Model recognizing players with poignant appreciation and acknowledgement. "I am really impressed by how willing everyone was to step out of their comfort zones; making something completely new on the spot, not knowing what was going to happen next, and being kind in the way you took it all lightly with laughter and joy!"

End the game and reflection time by acknowledging the group for its participation. "Thank you for taking the time to see others' greatness, and for seeing your own greatness!"

Elephant/Rabbit/Palm Tree

Set Up

This game works well for 20-40 players.

Arrange the players in a circle.

Teach the symbols/characters for this zany and exciting game, explaining that it always entails a reaction by three players working together to create those characters.

Demonstrate the Elephant: The center person extends his or her arms together out in front like a long trunk while players on either side hold their arms in curves to become big, floppy ears.

Then, demonstrate the Palm Tree: The center person extends his or her arms up overhead and outward, like a tall trunk that reaches for the sky, while players on either side create arching palm fronds with their arms.

Finally, demonstrate the Rabbit: The middle person makes big ears and big teeth while the person on each side thumps his or her outside foot.

Give participants a chance to practice each shape.

SEL Skills

- Relationship skills

- Social awareness

- Respect for social norms

- Managing stress

- Focus

- Self-regulation

Game On

1. The game begins with the leader standing in the center of the circle.

2. His or her job is to point to a person and say (1) Elephant, (2) Palm Tree, or (3) Rabbit.

3. The signified person and the people to his or her left and right must create the character before the leader can count to ten.

4. If the sequence is not done correctly or in time, the one who did not contribute in the prescribed way takes the place of the person in the center of the circle.

5. If the sequence is performed correctly, then the person in the center points to another player, until someone eventually makes a mistake.

Look for Greatness

Energize:

- Players attuning to body awareness and physical boundaries of self and others.

- Hearing the details of the instructions and being thoroughly prepared to begin game play.

- Willingness to follow directions; respecting someone else's authority.

- Being a leader with delight, decisiveness, and fairness.

- Thriving when being the center of attention.

- Accepting mistakes and making it fun.

- Being in control of personal reactions when managing stress.

- Playing all-out with openness and humor.

- Enthusiastically meeting challenges of effective communication and cooperation.

- Being flexible, responsive, and quick-thinking.

- Sensitivity to others' levels of willingness or capabilities.

- Physical creativity, agility, strength, and expressiveness.

- Encouragement of self and other players.

Clarity for Players

No touching in a disruptive or disrespectful manner.

No criticisms of anyone's creative choices.

No arguing with the person in the middle's expression of "Total-It-Power" (see below).

Total-It-Power

If there is disagreement or argument around whether someone has to replace the leader, introduce the concept of Total-It-Power.

Total-It-Power gives the person pointing in the center of the circle the authority to decide whether anyone has made a mistake. If that person says you made a mistake, you did, and you must replace them in the middle.

Generally, players won't mind being in the middle anyway. It is lots of fun!

This concept of Total-It-Power can be marvelously empowering. It gives the person in the middle the experience of having his or her opinion and judgment be fully respected.

Variations

Try adding more than one person in the middle to increase the action.

After a few minutes of play, add more prospective characters:

Supermodel: Middle person walks the runway; two side people take
   pictures.

Viking ship: Middle person makes Viking helmet with horns; the
   two outside people row.

Jell-O: Middle person jiggles; outside people join hands around the
   Jell-O to make the bowl.

Ideas for Reflection

Encourage group members to give one or two recognitions to self
   and/or others participating about what they observed or appreciated. Example: "I am so impressed with how fully engaged
   everyone was during the game, and how much respect you
   showed to each other... Is there anything you might do next
   time to notch it up?"

Ask the group for creative ideas for new symbols for the next time
   you play the game.

In a way, the game rewards mistakes; because then, a player gets
   to be in the middle and to be the center of attention! (This may
   not feel like a reward to all players, of course!) Ask, "How did
   it feel to make a mistake in the game? Was that fun to in the
   middle and the center of attention? If not, why did it feel uncomfortable?"

Connect the lesson to life:

   ● "How do you usually react when you make a mistake? Are
      you hard on yourself? If so, is there a way that you can reset
      yourself quickly and effectively? Is there an advantage in
      celebrating mistakes? Is it possible to learn anything new

without making mistakes?"

- "How can we celebrate our mistakes in a way that supports us in learning from them? Are we more accepting of others' mistakes than our own? If so, why? Where is it helpful in life to be able to honor and accept each other's mistakes?"

Recognize students for expressing the qualities identified at the start of the lesson: "I am really impressed with the way everyone honored the rule of Total-It-Power. I noticed the respect, support and focus you all gave the person in the center. That shows the empathy and respect you have for each other."

Support the conversation by asking what qualities they saw in others, in themselves, and in the group as a whole.

End the game and reflection time by acknowledging the group for its participation.

 **Mirroring**

Set Up

This partner game requires some space for pairs to move around in.

Have everyone choose partners and designate an A and a B.

Explain that everyone will take turns being a leader and follower.

Pair up with a participant to demonstrate. Designate yourself partner A and demonstrate holding up your hands and moving as though you were looking in a mirror. Let the other person mirror you. Then, instruct the volunteer to lead while you follow for the group to watch.

Demonstrate that as the activity progresses, the leader can add more movement with other parts of his or her body; can move through space; or can add sounds or facial expressions.

SEL Skills

- Relationship skills

- Social awareness

- Body awareness

- Creativity

- Focus

- Self-regulation

Game On

1. The facilitator calls out that A is the leader and B is the follower.

2. Switch leaders every ten to twenty seconds.

3. Remind people that they are responsible for their partner's success, which usually means moving slowly. (Be sure to demonstrate this.)

4. Tell participants that eye contact is 'home base.'

5. After a few changes, tell participants to continue moving and mirroring without either person being designated leader. Either person can initiate a movement at any time, while continuing to follow and be responsible for his or her partner's success.

6. In the last 30 seconds to a minute, ask pairs to find an elegant end to their dance.

7. Since everyone is with a partner, have each person share with their partner through quick pair-shares. "What made this game work well? What qualities of greatness did you

notice being expressed during the activity?" Then, intentionally find appreciative ways to nurture the hearts of the participants.

Look for Greatness

Energize:

- Embracing the game's simplicity and singularity of focus.

- Bravely being open to connection.

- Flexibility and enjoyment of sharing power by being able to flow back and forth between being a leader and a follower.

- Helping partner to feel seen, supported, and empowered by maintaining eye contact and fully following his or her movements.

- Slowing down, self-regulation, and positive awareness of others.

- Physical balance, focus, expressiveness, and gracefulness.

- Partners recognizing greatness in each other and mirroring that greatness.

Clarity for Players

No taking leadership when it is not your turn.

No criticisms of anyone's creative choices.

No moving too fast for your partner to follow you.

Let the players know that you trust them to follow the rules of the game as well as the general class rules; and that, if necessary, you will reset them so they can get right back into the game.

Variations

You can ask the players to do this with no sounds at all or encourage them to add sounds, depending on the energy you want to create in the room.

Many basic games are versions of mirroring. Try a simple game of Simon Says or Follow the Leader, where one person leads an activity and everyone else follows.

Try a game of "Yes, Let's." One person makes the suggestion, "Let's fly a kite." And everyone says "Yes, let's!" and everyone pretends to fly a kite. Then after 5-10 seconds, someone else says, "Let's bake a cake," and everyone says, "Yes, let's!" and everyone pretends to bake a cake.

Ideas for Reflection

Encourage group members to give one or two recognitions about what they observed or appreciated in themselves or others.

Sit with the group to talk about the two key concepts in this game: "How are you responsible for your partner's success?" "How is eye contact 'home base'?" "When were you reminded to keep good eye contact and did that make the game easier? If so, why?" "Where are some other areas in life where maintaining good eye contact is helpful?"

Connect the lesson to participants' own life experience: "This game gives you an experience of being supportive of your partner. Think of how it feels to be supportive when working on a project here in the classroom, or playing on a basketball team together. Where is it helpful in life to be supportive of your partner's success? How does it feel?"

Remind students of the qualities identified at the start of the lesson. Offer recognitions of those qualities with strong appreciation and acknowledgment as a model for students. Examples: "I am really impressed with how everyone moved slowly and was responsible for their partner's success. That takes composure, respect, and concentration. Those are qualities of greatness I see in you."

Support further conversation by asking what qualities students saw in each other, in themselves, and in the group as a whole. "What qualities did you notice that it took to maintain eye contact? To be a good leader and follower? Is there anyone who would like to acknowledge his or her partner in front of the whole group?"

End the game and reflection time by acknowledging the group for its participation.

 What Are You Doing?

Set Up

This game works well for 10-30 people.

Have everyone choose a partner.

Have the partners spread out in the space and decide which partner will go first.

Demonstrate the activity with a volunteer.

SEL Skills

- Relationship skills

- Social awareness

- Body awareness

- Creativity

- Support

● Respect

Game On

1. One person begins by acting out a simple action like brushing his or her teeth.

2. That person's partner asks, "[Student's name], what are you doing?"

3. The person brushing his or her teeth says something totally different from the action being performed, such as "I am flying a kite."

4. The person asking the question now acts out flying a kite.

5. The second person (the one who is flying the kite) is asked the question, "[Student's name], what are you doing?" and that student might say, "I am washing the dog."

6. That person acts out washing the dog...and back and forth it goes, around and around.

7. Switch partners and play again!

Look for Greatness

Energize:

● Having fun with simplicity.

● Supporting the other players in doing well by choosing approachable situations to act out.

● Inventiveness, willingness, and enthusiasm to jump in to act out what is suggested.

● Quick-thinking, brilliant imagination and creativity when coming up with scene ideas.

- Encouragement of other players.

- Awareness of boundaries and respect toward and working within others' limits.

- Bravery in acting in front of other people.

- Silliness, humor, jubilance and joy.

- Inventive use of the body.

- Self-control, patience, and appreciation when other players are acting.

Clarity for Players

No making suggestions that are overly embarrassing to your partner.

No criticisms of anyone's creative choices.

No speaking out or interrupting others when instructions are being given.

Let players know that you trust them to follow the rules of the game as well as the general class rules, as well as respecting their partners' requests, and that you will offer resets to help them get back on purpose.

Variations

It's fun to make two offers at the same time, still remembering to keep it simple. "I am eating an ice cream cone and singing opera." Or, "I am riding my bike and laughing." ("I am playing my ukulele while fighting an awesome, disgusting T-Rex who is trying to eat me" may be a little too difficult; see "Dare to be average," above.)

This game can be also played in a circle with one person doing the action and the person on his or her left asking the question,

"What are you doing?" and going around the circle. This is a great opportunity for everyone to observe the creativity of each person in the circle.

Try bringing two people up to play the game in front of the group. Afterwards, ask the group what qualities they saw expressed in the players: kindness, playfulness, bravery, humor, or joy.

Try asking players to add an adverb to their offer once they are comfortable with this game. Give a few examples: "What are you doing?" "I am running *awkwardly.*" Or, "I am playing with my dog *wildly.*" Or, "I am laughing *uncontrollably.*" Or, "I am washing the dishes *sadly* or *angrily.*"

Ideas for Reflection

Ask the group questions:

- "What did you notice about each person's ability to be spontaneous and playful?"

- "What made it possible to come up with creative ideas?"

- "What were your favorite parts of the game?"

Connect the lesson to their lives:

- "Where is it helpful in life to be able to make your partner look good?"

- "How does it feel to play with a partner doing something so simple and fun?"

Ask players to reflect upon their own contributions: "What is something that you did to make your partner look good or feel supported? What was that like? What qualities do you have that helped you do that?"

Remind students of the qualities identified at the start of the lesson. Model giving recognition to students with strong appreciation and acknowledgment. Example: "I am really impressed with the inventiveness and playfulness everyone showed during this game. I noticed the willingness to try a new game, and the cleverness and expressiveness in people's choices." Support the conversation by asking what qualities they saw in others, in themselves, and in the group as a whole.

End the game and reflection time by acknowledging group members for their participation.

 Whoosh

Set Up

This game works well for 8 – 20 players.

Start with everyone standing in a circle.

SEL Skills

- Relationship skills
- Social awareness
- Body awareness
- Creativity
- Focus
- Self-regulation

Game On

1. Show the group how to pass a wave around the circle—by moving their hands as if passing a little wave in one direc-

tion, saying "Whoosh," as they do.

2. Pass the whooshing wave around the circle a couple of times.

3. Let them know you are going to add several other elements as the game progresses.

4. Add the "Whoa!" command: when the whoosh comes along, players can elect to raise one hand and say, "Whoa," which stops the Whoosh and sends it back in the direction from which it came.

5. Play this for a bit. Notice that the Whoosh can get stuck, with people on each side of the whoosher saying "Whoa" each time it comes to them.

6. Add the "Zap" element: players can choose to Zap a Whoosh across the circle by slapping their hands together at another player. Have the Zapper make eye contact with the person they are zapping and make sure to say "Zap" nice and loud. The recipient of the Zap now has two choices: either sending the Zap to someone else or to start a new Whoosh in either direction. (There is no Whoa-ing a Zap.)

7. Play for a bit with these three rules in place.

8. Then, add "Groove-a-licious." Players can choose, when the Whoosh comes to them, to wave their arms in front of themselves like dancers getting groovy and say, "Groove-a-licious!" Everyone else mirrors that person's sound and movement.

9. Then, add a *non sequitur* option: when the Whoosh comes to you, you can do anything you want for a few seconds and everyone has to mirror you. After either a Groove-a-licious or a *non sequitur,* that same person must then get the game going with either a Whoosh or a Zap.

THE GREATNESS OF RISK-TAKING, CREATIVITY AND FOLLOWING THE RULES

10. Play a little more!

11. Finally, add the "Freak Out." When the Whoosh comes to you, say, "Freak out!" and everyone then has to run around and change places in the circle. The player who said "Freak Out" then starts the Whoosh going again with one of the other choices.

Look for Greatness
Energize:

- Sharing being the center of attention with the rest of the group.

- Self-expression, exuberance, and joy in contributing to the game.

- Responding cooperatively to the movement prompts and being supportive of others' decisions.

- Persistence with the game even when feeling uncomfortable about being watched.

- Bodily safety and control, respecting other players' physical space.

- Inventiveness and creativity with the creation of movements.

- Willingness to be silly.

- Making independent and individual choices.

- Being attentive and aware.

Clarity for Players

No taking the focus of the game when it isn't your turn.

No taking the focus for more than only a few seconds when it is your turn.

No bumping into anyone or using your body unsafely.

No interrupting when directions are being given.

Let the players know that you trust them to follow the rules of the game as well as the general class rules; and that, if necessary, you will reset them so they can get right back into the game.

Variations

This is one example of a circle game that involves passing energy. Look for more games that incorporate the passing of energy. Kids love them.

This game has many rules; simplify it by just doing the "Whoosh" and "Whoa" portion of this game the first time you play, and then add in a new rule each time you bring the game back.

With younger children or special needs populations, you can designate only a couple of players who can say the "Whoa," thus giving those few chosen students "Whoa-power."

Try just passing the "Zap" around as a fun warm-up by itself, or use the triad of sounds "Zip, Zap, Zop," with players having to say the correct word from the sequence when the energy shoots to them.

You can just pass a sound and motion around the circle. You can then have each player change the motion and sound slightly as it comes to him or her; it will morph hilariously as it goes around the circle.

Have the group make up its own sounds and movements that represent the passing, stopping, and zapping of the energy: maybe *Zip, Stop, Boing,* or *Wham-a-lama-ding dong!*

Ideas for Reflection

Encourage group members to give one or two recognitions to self and/or others participating about what they observed or appreciated: "I am so impressed by how focused and patient everyone was during the game."

Ask the group questions like:

- "What did you see happening in this game?"
- "What did we do? What did it take to do these things?"
- "How does it feel to be a part of group all having fun together?"
- "What made the game fun and full of laughter?"
- "What made it easy and possible in this game to maintain focus?"
- "What were your favorite parts of the game?"

Connect the lesson to their lives:

- "Where is it helpful in life to be able to allow others to have the focus and attention while we observe?"
- "How does it feel to be supportive of other people's creativity?"
- "Can you think of examples where being focused and giving the focus to others happen in life: being in an audience, watching a play, listening to a speech? What qualities does it take to give focus to others?"
- "How does it feel when others do not pay attention to you

when it is your turn to have the focus? What qualities of greatness are required when you take the focus – when you are the center of attention for a few moments or more?"

Model giving recognitions to players with strong appreciation and acknowledgment: "I really enjoyed the feeling of everyone being in a circle together, respecting each other and allowing each person to have the focus during their turn...The variety and inventiveness that people showed in creating fun non sequitur movements was so entertaining." Support the conversation by asking what qualities they saw in others, in themselves and in the group as a whole.

End the game and reflection time by acknowledging the group for its participation.

Acknowledgements and Resets
for Improvisation Games

How do we, as adults, create environments that foster learning, safety, and harmony, while still allowing the play drive that sparks creative expression, enthusiasm – even a kind of wildness?

Nurtured Heart Play is a container created by specific boundaries that holds more chaotic energies in check by channeling those same energies to greatness. It acknowledges that firmly held rules and boundaries are the magical ingredients that allow kids to be playful and serious at the same time. And there is seriousness in keeping everyone safe, physically and mentally. Learning to respect the boundaries and feelings of others is the cornerstone of emotional intelligence and executive functioning. Solid rules also set the stage for the easy flow of recognitions, even extending to the greatness of the group as a whole – because *any rule that is being followed can be given recognitions.* Much of the training in improvisational theater and social play has been based on saying "yes" to what arises and going with it; with being optimistic and positive. Does this conflict with the stance of Absolutely No? In a word: No.

Many of the activities and exercises in Nurtured Heart Play are drawn from improvisational theater games, where one of the guiding principles is to say "yes" to what the other actors offer and add to it. So the phrase, "Yes, and..." becomes the springboard to good improv experiences for players and for the audience: these games are all about accepting others' ideas as the reality of the current scene, and then building on it. This fundamental guiding principle of improv theater is very much in alignment with Stand Two. Saying "yes, and" is congruent with energizing success.

This is a skill that translates into most other aspects of our lives: saying "yes, and..." instead of "no, but..." feels good and yields all kinds of new discoveries in every moment. Having a lighthearted, playful attitude and a willingness to say yes to people's playfulness in the daily flow of life can be an amazing interpersonal support to us all. Making silly faces, laughing at our mistakes, playing a word game while driving in the car, smiling at the checkout person in the store and wishing them a great day are all examples of how any of us can be the person who finds more joy in each moment.

Another guiding principle in improv is: always do your best to make your partner look good. In this way, these games are all about helping others succeed and express their greatness. What a perfect way to move into acknowledging the people you are playing with; seeing who they are in each moment and saying "Yes and..." to them through sharing with them the qualities they are exhibiting in relation to the game and the other players.

Attentive improv game play gives abundant evidence to create a story about a person's greatness. Saying, *"Yes, I see you may be feeling nervous about participating, and you are being quiet and respectful while processing your feelings. That shows me you are patient with yourself, you are giving others space to enjoy taking their turn, you are observing your classmates' roles in the game, and you are being thoughtful about how you will participate."* Recognitions rooted in the reality of what we see creates opportunity to see the beauty of that reality, and lets you invent a great story from there. "That shows me you are extremely peaceful in how you process emotions, and I saw you fearlessly stay part of the group while you were doing that important inner work. That reveals to me the greatness of your being purposeful, peaceful and fearless."

These games are a great place to look for acceptance of the way the game has progressed; for players being present and responding creatively and positively to the current situation; and for seeing the greatness in other players' choices. It might show up as a player giving verbal encouragement, readjusting to meet someone where his or her capabilities are or willingness lie, a smile, or simply watching without judgment. This reveals the player coming to the game with openness.

Here are examples of how recognition can be effortlessly incorporated into improv games. Be mindful of the challenges players may be confronting in order to be part of the game, and how they are overcoming them. They are being vulnerable and silly; they are sensitively and encouragingly witnessing others' imaginations and emotions. They are inspiring creativity in others. This takes a lot of presence, bravery, and flexibility in each new moment. Capitalize on these vulnerable moments to nourish their greatness. Make all moments into shining accomplishments.

Play is a time when people are present, aware of themselves and those around them, and responding to each other to cultivate a situation of fun. This back-and-forth constructing of experience is a factory of relationship; watch carefully and see all the ways players encourage each other simply by sharing enjoyment in the successes and limitations of each person's body, imagination, and emotions. It is a time to witness and make light of humanness. A player showing willingness to do this is revealing his or her deep capabilities for the greatness of compassion, empathy, kindness, patience, attentiveness, vulnerability, individuality, courage, and so on.

All the kindling is already there. Each person has these qualities. Watching for and acknowledging glimmers of greatness may be all that it takes to set them ablaze with the knowledge of the magnitude of their character.

Resetting players is key to creating feelings of safety and respected boundaries during play, especially during play like theater games that ask players to reveal their imagination, creativity and humor, all of which can be tender pieces of our humanness. Therefore, honor your playmates' bravery by providing with them solid parameters of no judging others, no laughing where it is not appropriate, no physical contact when not appropriate, and no interrupting. Be clear at the beginning of the game what is expected of each player, and even ask for suggestions of what would make people feel safe.

As game facilitator, watch for rules being broken, insert a reset, and immediately use it as an opportunity to build up the feeling of safety and collaboration. In these moments there are players not breaking the rules, energize that! Energize any player who breaks a rule as soon as he or she reenters the game constructively. These are perfect opportunities to renew a player to the greatness of *who he or she really is,* as a person who can: (1) reset successfully, and (2) successfully and respectfully stay on purpose and follow the rules. This takes inner power, resolve, determination, and great intention.

Our culture easily slips into giving children credit for poor choices, and this is often done in very energized ways. NHA is a way of giving great credit for the wonderful choice of clarity in adhering to the rules. We are never NOT choosing.

Freely give credit for good judgment and decisions reflected by positive behaviors. Keep up the vibrancy in seeing the positive choices players are making. This reinforces relationship with positivity, making the reset a simple shift of energy and not a big affair or opportunity for relationship.

Active Recognitions are direct observations and will register to the child as being seen, meaningful, and valued.

"John, I saw you jump up and be the first one to participate."

"Sue, you are sitting here waiting your turn."

"Tim, you did not touch or push anyone as you walked up!"

"Carol, you told me you didn't want to be here today, yet you're participating in the game and you're not complaining."

"Wow, the three of you were on it! Your eyes were on Jamie and when she pointed to you; you made your formation in seconds. And then you held it."

"Mariah, you watched as each player took their turn around the circle until it was your turn again."

"Kyle, thank you for contributing your part to the game at just the right time. I saw you instantly engage with precision timing."

Experiential Recognitions are acknowledgements of great qualities seen through the evidence of a person's actions; what is seen supports the truth of the qualities being recognized. These can be combined beautifully with Proactive Recognitions or used alone.

"Rachel, I hear you encouraging your neighbor to participate! Being outgoing to help your classmates shows you have great care and thoughtfulness."

"Janet, I noticed you created a really unique new movement for the game. You helped everyone to have laughter and enjoyment."

"Peter, I saw that a classmate was bugging you during the game, and you continued to play without bugging him back. You have relentless determination and self-control!"

"Joe, you kept up your role in the game the entire time, even when it got tiring. You didn't stop, and that shows your greatness of perseverance and dependability."

"Thank you, Joseph, for your unique idea for how to make the game better. I can see you were thoughtfully and compassionately observing what your classmates needed during the game to enjoy it more."

"Sarah, you are so wise for perceiving Robert's creativity, and so brave for acknowledging him for his contribution to the game. Thank you."

"Freddy, the way you got in front of the class with so much vigor and energy really gave a gift of entertainment and camaraderie to the class. To take the game beyond what was expected of you shows me you understand the power of making people laugh...and you did it in a positive way, which demonstrated your choice of excellent judgment and restraint. Thank you for being a model for the class of how to be silly and creative at an appropriate time, and in a way that made everyone feel uplifted!"

"Sarah, you've never played this game before, and you jumped right in with a smile on your face and excitement in your voice. You have the greatness of fun and openness to trying new things. I also noticed how the energy flowed between you and your partner. You both seemed to play off the others and have fun doing it. You both have the greatness of partnership and support."

Proactive Recognitions are appreciations given when the rules are not being broken, emphasizing the qualities it takes to not break the rules.

"Galen, I greatly appreciate that you are following the rules right now. You could have made your partner uncomfortable, but you didn't. You were supportive and made it fun for you both. That shows me your maturity and kindness."

"Caleb, you did not lean on anyone during the game. You modeled the rule about not leaning on others, and that shows your leadership and determination. Those are great qualities I see in you."

"Many of you had to wait a long time before it was

your group's turn. Not once did you touch, push, or talk to anyone around you. You could have done all of those things but you chose not to. You have the greatness of self-control and determination to follow the rules."

"As we were playing the game, the three of you did not disturb those around you with your voices, or by being aggressive or fooling around with each other. None of you missed your turn or disrupted the flow of the game. That takes commitment by each of you to follow the rules, along with the greatness of enthusiasm and making a positive community. I love that you all are able to have fun in such a mature way."

"Sharon, you didn't keep raising your hand when you weren't chosen to go first. You are very wise and trusting."

"Hal, even though I can see that you look tempted to respond to your neighbor distracting you, I see you holding back your words even though your body is facing his direction. You are giving a momentous effort of determination and self-control! All of that hard work shows me you are mighty and independent in knowing who you are!"

Creative Recognitions celebrate the following of rules and responding appropriately to clear requests, as well set up situations where the child can easily succeed in complying.

"Shelby, just as I am asking you to walk over into the line, I see you already heading in that direction. Thank you for being aware of the other players and what is needed for this moment of the game. That shows me you are very perceptive and wanting to be collaborative in playing."

"Alice, I can see you thinking about speaking your part for the next part of the game, even though you are nervous. I applaud you for feeling your feelings and being brave in the face of them to help continue the game. That shows me you trust that all of us support you."

"I need a volunteer for the middle...Julian, you raised your hand as soon as I asked and stood there quietly until I called on you. I appreciate your willingness to volunteer so quickly and respectfully!"

"I see you all picking up the materials as you have sensed the game is ending. Thank you for helping clean up! You read my mind...I didn't even have to ask. That is the greatness of taking initiative."

Resets for Improv Games

"Tom, reset."... "Tom, you stopped being silly, and that takes self-control and resolve. Thank you for resetting so well."

"Laura, reset."... "Laura, thank you for completing your reset. You're now doing your part in the game without leaning on your neighbor. That takes respectfulness, to reset to following that rule."

"Ethan, great reset! I saw your friend fall on you and I

saw you start to push him back, and then you decided not to. You went back to playing instead. Great resiliency and intention!"

"Kyle, thank you for resetting. I see you looking to what your classmates are doing to help you get right back to playing."

"Ann, you stopped putting your hands on Lisa and are now keeping them by your side or in front of you. I see your control."

"Becca, you chose to immediately change your mind after you started to make a face; I saw you think about it and stop. You are greatly in charge of your emotions and body. You are also kind...you knew it makes your classmates feel good to see your support. You reset yourself. You are showing the greatness of leadership."

"Zach, you reset after I asked you to take your turn. You responded by being joyful at getting to be in the game and excited to contribute."

MINDFULNESS GAMES:

THE GREATNESS OF BEING PRESENT AND FOCUSED

Nurtured Heart Play is a wonderful way to teach and practice presence, focus, and mindfulness. The whole process of giving acknowledgements brings a mindful quality to any activity; these games make this link between positive acknowledgement and mindfulness more explicit, offering powerful support toward learning to be truly in the moment in a spirit of gratitude and joy. When you verbalize what you are seeing in other people, they get a reflection of what they are doing and a chance to self-appreciate and hone their own focus.

Anyone who has attempted a mindfulness practice like meditation knows that honing your attention can be challenging. Touching into silence and emptiness for a few moments usually gives way to a flurry of thought or outside distraction! What many novices don't know about this is that all the mental chatter and distraction is part of the process of learning to be mindful, as is resetting from those things back to present awareness. Nurtured Heart adds an element of discernment, where we particularly learn to reset from negative mental chatter (worry, misery, doubt – what Howard Glasser calls "WMDs") to an appreciation of the positive in the present moment.

Laugh about how easily attention wanders; delight in the attempts made; acknowledge the greatness in what happens. Value the process of growth. Reset players when needed, knowing it is just a momentary pause so the player can remember their focus and shift away from distractions. Welcome players back after resets, because it takes courage to trust in rejoining the team and being included equally again.

 ## Overload

Set Up

This game works for groups from four to 30+.

Have everyone count off into groups of four and have each member of the group choose a number, one through four, so there is only one of each number in each group.

Number One will be the first person to be the focus of the other three players in their group. Number Two stands to his or her left, Number Three stands in front of him or her, and Number Four stands to his or her right.

SEL Skills

- Focus

- Emotional regulation

- Managing stress

- Confidence

Game On

1. Number One is the "overloaded" player whose job it is to answer questions and mirror movements supplied by the other players in her or his group.

2. Number Two asks simple, personal, fun questions; slowly at first, then faster as the game progresses. (What color is

the sky? What street do you live on? What is your favorite flavor of ice cream?)

3. Number Three makes simple movements that Number One must mirror.

4. Number Four asks simple math questions: 2+8, 5x6, and so on.

5. The two questioners alternate their asking of questions.

6. As the game starts, the questioners ask questions slowly. As the game goes on, they speed up. If an answer is not correct or forthcoming, or if the mirroring is not being followed, then that person repeats the question or the mirroring person reminds the person to focus on them. The overload player can stop when sufficiently overloaded.

Look for Greatness
Energize:

- Great attention and ability to focus on one task at a time.

- Relaxedness in receiving lots of stimulus.

- Tolerance of chaos.

- Persistence and determination to try again.

- Enjoyment of the struggle; seeing there is playfulness in stress.

- Fortitude and centeredness.

- Self-resetting and consideration to allow other players to reset to be effective in the game.

- Gentleness and appropriateness in giving the questions and prompts.

- Focus on prescribed task to give or respond to.

Clarity for Players

No loud noises near anyone's ear.

No moving so fast that the person doing the mirroring cannot keep up.

No inappropriate or embarrassing questions.

Let the players know that you have faith they will be able to follow the rules of the game as well as the general class rules; and that, if necessary, you will reset them so they can get right back into the game.

Ideas for Reflection

This game plays with the concept of multi-tasking and helping the players deal with stress under conditions of increasing complexity. If your group understands the concept of resetting one's self in stressful situations, discuss it in that context, or take this opportunity to introduce the self-reset in this experiential context.

Encourage group members to give one or two recognitions to self and/or others about what they observed or appreciated. Give a recognition yourself, first, to set the tone. For example: "John, I noticed how you reset when the questioning was getting to be too much. I saw you take a deep breath and pause, and then you continued to answer a few more questions before you said you were done. You decided when you were done, not letting your stressful feelings take you over. You used your greatness of calmness and restraint to move forward in the way the YOU wanted to."

Let the group know that the ability to shift attention as required in this game takes focus, concentration, and patience. Discuss and acknowledge their successes in this, as well as their successes in constructively managing the frustration the activity brings up:

- "How did it feel to try something that seemed to be easy at first and then became harder and harder?"

- "At what point did the stress become more difficult?"

- "Did you notice how your body responded? Did you notice how your thoughts responded?"

- Connect the lesson to life:

- "Where are there times in life when many things are happening at once and you have to pay attention to one important thing? Driving a car, perhaps?"

- "What are the skills necessary to maintain focus on one thing at a time and also to shift focus? Where do you see this in life? Doctors, EMTs, athletes in competition?"

- "Have you ever started something that seemed easy that then got to be too hard? When did you know you needed to reset or stop?"

End the game and reflection time by acknowledging the group for its exceptional participation.

Shake and Babble

Set Up

This game works well for groups of any size.

Have participants spread out so each has his/her own space.

Tell participants to stand and put their feet firmly on the ground: "Imagine your feet are frozen in place like someone has poured concrete over them, or that your feet are giant suction cups stuck firmly to the floor."

SEL Skills

- Focus

- Emotional regulation

- Managing stress

Game On

1. Tell the players, "Start shaking your whole body. Shake your arms; shake your torso; shake your hips; shake your head. Imagine you're a big bowl of jelly, or you're a rag doll, and a giant has picked you up and is shaking you..."

2. Once everyone is shaking, add the element of sound: "Now, add some sounds—whatever wants to come out of you! Babble, hum, sing..."

3. Try appointing one or two youth to un-stick themselves from their spots, bringing their shaking, babbling selves closer to more inhibited students to add to their energy.

Look for Greatness

Energize:

- Willingness to let go of insecurities about being silly.

- Facing the possibility of embarrassment.

- Being incredibly responsive to how the body wants to move and make noise.

- Engaging with other players to create comfort in community.

- Helping other players to enjoy the game by lending their energy.

- Fully inhabiting one's body with joy and relaxation.

- Making big, interesting sounds, and shaking without inhibition.

- Awareness of the energy expressed and released.

- Awareness of personal need for energetic release.

Clarity for Players

No judgments or negative comments about anyone's physical expression.

No physical touching.

No unkind or derogatory words.

Let players know that you have faith they will be able to follow the rules of the game as well as the general class rules; and that, if necessary, you will reset them so they can get right back into the game.

Variations

Everyone walks around the room while shaking and babbling.

Babble/shake face-offs: Have players walk up to others and shake and babble while facing off with them.

Allow players to yell and scream, too, as long as you are in a space where lots of noise is OK.

Have players close their eyes while shaking and babbling to see how that feels.

Ideas for Reflection

Remind students of the qualities identified at the start of the lesson. Model acknowledging those qualities in the players with strong appreciation. Support the conversation by asking what

CHAPTER SEVEN ♥ MINDFULNESS GAMES

qualities they saw in others, in themselves and in the group as a whole.

Save time to hear from the group:

- "What was that game like for each of you?"

- "Were there parts that were more fun or easier or more difficult than others?"

- "What did you do to make it fun and successful? What qualities did it take to do these things? Attention, determination, playfulness, enthusiasm?"

Encourage group members to give one or two recognitions to self and/or others participating about what they observed or appreciated. Create momentum for this by modeling as needed: "I am so impressed by how fully invested everyone was in expressing themselves, and how much fun everyone was having."

Discuss how the group's energy was shifted by this activity. Ask the group for other creative ideas about how to shift energy when this seems called for (when stress is high, for example), and how this is a way of resetting:

- "Let's take a walk around the room!"

- "Let's just shake out our hands really hard while sitting at our desks."

- "Let's turn to a neighbor and babble for 30 seconds!"

- "Let's stand up, do a 30 second dance, and get right back to work."

This activity provides a great opportunity to talk about awareness of energy in the body. Ask students to reflect directly on their body sensations:

- "What changes did you notice in your body after shaking and babbling?"

- "Do you feel different sensations in your hands, in your legs, in your face, throat or chest after doing the shaking?"

- "How did it feel to make sounds that may be considered silly? Was that easy to do, or hard?"

Connect the body awareness aspect of this lesson to life – in particular, how to use/shift body energy to reset:

- "What experiences have you had of bringing awareness to the energy of your body?"

- "What are ways that you shift energy in your everyday life? Taking a walk, putting on music and dancing, or going outside and playing?"

- "Can you remember a time when you felt frustrated or antsy and then did something and it shifted? What are other ways that you reset yourself?"

- End the game and reflection time by acknowledging the group for its participation.

Shake and Stop

Set Up

This game works well for any size group.

First, acknowledge any pent-up energy in the group: "Wow! I can tell you all have a lot of energy in your bodies right now. Let's play with that feeling."

SEL Skills

- Focus

- Emotional regulation

- Managing stress

Game On

1. Tell the group, "Right now, while sitting in your chairs, go ahead and shake your whole body. When I say stop, let's see how still we can be for three seconds."

2. Then, have them shake again and instruct, "This time, let's be still for five seconds."

3. Ask, "What's the record we can set for today? Can we be still for 10 seconds?" and so on.

4. As you wrap up the activity, have participants take a moment in stillness to notice what is happening in their bodies.

Look for Greatness
Energize:

- Trusting in the acceptance of the group to let down inhibitions.

- Creating space for that trust by not judging others.

- Delighting in silliness.

- Using intention to add to the physical release, which shows determination, enthusiasm, and both emotional and mental openness.

- Letting go of pent-up energy.

- Careful attention to how the body responds to shaking.

- Gentleness and fervor with the body.

- Appreciating and relishing the experience and significance of relaxation in the body.

Clarity for Players

No physical touching.

No yelling or loud noises.

No judgments or negative comments about anyone's physical expressions.

No arguing, roughhousing, bad words, or breaking any other of the general classroom rules while we are playing.

Let the players know that you have faith they will be able to follow the rules of the game as well as the general class rules; and that, if necessary, you will reset them so they can get right back into the game.

Variations

Have participants stand up to shake at their desks or chairs.

Focus on a specific body part: "Let's shake our arms!" or "Let's shake our legs!"

Follow the leader: allow individual participants to lead the group in shaking a particular body part and shaking it in a certain way.

Have the players try closing their eyes while shaking and stopping to see how that feels.

Ideas for Reflection

Help participants reflect on the activity with basic questions like:

- "What did we just do?"

- "Was it fun?"

- "Did you like being still or moving more?"

- "What did it take to do that over and over again and for longer periods of time?"

- "Did you know you could do that?"

- "How does it feel to know you can do that in the future?"

Remind students of the qualities identified at the start of the lesson. Did they see what they predicted? Model by recognizing students with strong appreciation and acknowledgement: "So even though you didn't want to or like to stop, you did. What qualities of greatness did that take?" Support the conversation by asking what qualities they saw in others, in themselves and in the group as a whole.

Ask the players to offer greatness appreciations to each other – a great way to end the activity and to anchor learning for everyone. Try it as a quick popcorn-style sharing with the raising of hands, or go around the circle to let each person offer words of appreciation. Encourage group members to give one or two recognitions to self and to others participating about what they observed or appreciated. Create momentum for this by modeling as needed. Example: "I am so impressed by the willingness and exuberance everyone exhibited during this activity. You all really went for it. Those are great qualities I see in you."

Connect the lesson to their lives:

- "Are there times in life where you have pent-up energy? What do you do to move that energy? Take a walk, play a game, dance?"

- "What are your favorite and most effective ways to move

your energy?"

- "Are there times in life where you need to be still? When do you like to be still? When is stillness good?"

End the game and reflection time by acknowledging the group for its participation.

 **Distraction Game**

Materials
A chair set up in front of the group.

Set Up
This game works well for 2-30 people. It lends itself well to being played in any environment where people can be seated and observing.

Explain that you will be asking a volunteer to come and sit in the chair to be the "object person." His or her only responsibility in the game is to sit still and focus on his or her breath without being distracted.

Explain to the group that it can clap, bang around the room, ask questions, rustle paper, make other noises, or try anything else within the rules of the group or the classroom to try and distract the person in the chair.

Make sure that participants know they cannot make any loud noises near the person's ears, and that they cannot physically touch the person.

Take the seat yourself first to demonstrate how it's done within the given rules.

SEL Skills

- Focus

- Emotional regulation

- Managing stress

- Controlling impulses

Game On

1. Have the group do whatever it can to distract you as you sit in the chair.

2. Once the players have taken about a minute or so to try and distract you (hopefully, you will be able to demonstrate remaining calm and still despite all attempted distractions), pause the game to recognize the group for a quality you wish to appreciate – such as its creativity in coming up with clever ways to try to distract you!

3. Choose a new "distractee" and play a few more times; take time for reflection after each round of the game.

This activity can be uproariously funny. Observers can enjoy and build on each other's attempts to create effective distractions. The more serious side of this learning experience lies in the fact that the ability to remain focused and grounded in the face of lots of distractions is an important life skill. Through this lighthearted look at distraction, we can then enter into deeper conversations about how to manage stress and deal with the moment-to-moment distractions that happen for all of us. This is an excellent way for the players to feel into the importance of this skill – to learn and to experiment with different breathing techniques and mindfulness practices, and how to reset themselves continually throughout the day. This simple act of resetting oneself takes practice and mindfulness. Doing this in a fun way brings a playful awareness to this simple, yet profoundly important skill for everyone to learn.

Look for Greatness
Energize:

- Creative and crafty distractions.

- Enthusiastic energy.

- Unwavering focus, either in trying to distract or not be distracted!

- Calm breathing and maintaining softness during the chaos.

- Complete respect of the rules, recognizing the need to honor the distractee's personal boundaries.

- Lightheartedly being serious about succeeding at the game.

- Managing stress reactions, and being okay with failing to keep them in complete control.

- Confidence in remaining centered; fortitude, resolve, and nobility.

- Persistence and perseverance.

- Determination and concentration.

- Personal power!

Clarity for Players
No loud noises near anyone's ear.

No physical touching.

No unkind or derogatory words.

No disrupting the physical space, like knocking over chairs, in your attempts to distract the distractee.

Let the players know that you have faith they will be able to follow the rules of the game as well as the general class rules; and that, if necessary, you will reset them so they can get right back into the game.

Variations

Everyone in the room sits in stillness while one person walks around the room, making noises and trying to distract anyone in the group.

Add more "distractors" and have them move around the room to try to distract people in chairs.

Ideas for Reflection

Remind students of the qualities identified at the start of the lesson. Did they see what they predicted? Model by recognizing students with strong appreciation and acknowledgment. Examples: "I am really impressed by the creativity people used in their attempts to distract the person while not invading their personal space. Also, the concentration and presence it took to not get distracted showed a lot of resourcefulness, focus and mindfulness!"

Support the conversation by asking what qualities they saw in others, in themselves and in the group as a whole.

Encourage group members to give one or two recognitions to self and/or others participating about what they observed or appreciated. Create momentum for this by modeling as needed. Example: "I am very impressed by the determination it took to not be distracted during the game."

Open up discussion in the group with questions like:

- "What challenge did you encounter during the game?"

- "What did you see your fellow players doing well?"

- "What were methods you used to stay focused during the game?"

Connect the lesson to players' lives:

- "When in your life do you need to maintain attention, inspiration, and purpose and not be distracted?"

- "Have you been successful at school in not being distracted, or doing your homework at home while your siblings are playing or there is noise around?"

- "How about shooting a free throw in a basketball game and the crowd is making noise?"

- "What strategies have you used successfully?"

- "Can you see the importance of learning how to do this?"

End the game and reflection time by acknowledging the group for its participation.

 Freeze Dance

Materials
A portable music player or sound system.

Set Up
This game works well for any size group.

Have everyone spread out in the room, taking enough space to properly bust a move.

Put on some great dance music.

Tell students not to touch each other during this game and to maintain a small cushion of personal space throughout.

Game On

1. Put on some great dance music; let everyone begin dancing.

2. Stop the music! This is the cue for everyone to freeze.

3. After a few seconds, start the music again; dancing begins anew.

4. Pause the music again.

5. Vary the amount of time between the pauses of music and the length of the pauses.

6. Challenge players to see how long they can hold their poses during each succeeding stop: "Wow, that's great! Everyone held still for six seconds. Let's go for 10 seconds this time!"

7. Emphasize holding as absolutely still as possible during the freezes and moving with (safe) abandon during the un-frozen periods of the game.

SEL Skills

- Focus

- Emotional regulation

- Managing stress

- Controlling impulses

- Social awareness

Look for Greatness

Energize:

- Honoring other players' personal space.

- Taking care of personal physical boundaries.

- Balancing kinesthetic awareness and letting go into the flow of the dance.

- Celebrating individuality, creative expression, and enthusiastically expanding energy.

- Cultivating mastery of stillness and concentration.

- Willpower, determination, and perseverance to remain still.

- Mindfulness during the game to respond to the changing environment and prompts.

- Utilizing useful tools to be still.

- Creating a communal sense of emotional safety by encouraging and not judging teammates.

- Embracing space, music, and rhythm to create an improvised dance.

Clarity for Players

No physical touching during dancing.

No bumping into anyone.

No negative comments about anyone's dancing.

No arguing, roughhousing, bad words, or breaking any other of the general rules while we are playing.

Let players know that you have faith they will be able to follow the rules of the game as well as the general group rules; and that, if necessary, you will reset them so they can get right back into the game.

Variations

Freeze statues: Once the music stops, participants each join with another person to make a partner statue. Once partners have chosen each other, one will pose and the other will complete the statue by filling in negative space around the other partner's shape. This can be done without touching.

Three-person or four-person statues are also an option: When the music stops, players join with a set number of people; they'll have three or four seconds to freeze in a statue. "Try statues of four!"

Play musical hugs. If you are in a setting where hugging is permitted, when the music stops, players hug in groups of whatever number the leader calls out. "Hug in fives!"

Invite youth with unique dance moves to teach their moves to their classmates.

Ideas for Reflection

This game presents a great opportunity to talk about personal space and about how good it feels to have that space honored. It can also be a great lesson in mindfulness: have participants reflect on how they maintain stillness. Do they focus on their breath? Do they lock eyes with a friend? Or do they stare at some point in the room?

Give players a chance to share what the experience of playing this game was like for them. Continue to build acknowledgments by encouraging group members to give one or two recognitions to self and/or others participating about what they observed or appreciated. Take appreciation to the level of greatness:

- "What was great about the game and each other?"

- "Is there anything you might do next time to notch it up?"

This game plays with the concepts of movement, creative expression, and stillness, so focus on these concepts in your de-brief:

- "How did it feel to be dancing, then stopping? Did you find it difficult to stop and be still?"

- "What helped you to be still? Were you able to stay frozen by way of concentration, willpower, determination, or perseverance?"

- "Did it feel good to dance? What forms of creative expression make you feel good?"

- "Do you sometimes worry about how others are judging you when you are dancing?"

Connect the lesson to life, where the ability to shift from action to stillness is a valuable tool:

- "Are there times at school or at home that you have to stop doing something whether you are ready or not; in other words, to reset yourself to stillness?"

- "What are some examples of your successes resetting to stillness today?"

- "What qualities does that ability show?"

Resetting from embarrassment in order to freely self-express is another valuable skill: "Are there times in life when it is useful to persevere through feelings of embarrassment? When have you done this well?"

End the game and reflection time by acknowledging the group for its exceptional participation.

 **Hula Hoop Pass**

Materials

At least one hula hoop per group.

Set Up

This game works well with 8-20 players. You can split a larger group into two or more smaller groups.

If space requires, you can put a smaller group inside a larger one.

Link up so the entire group is holding hands, with a hula hoop around the gripped hands of any two people in the circle.

Explain that the goal of this game is to get the hoop to travel around the entire circle without breaking a link.

Decide which direction the hula hoop will go.

SEL Skills

- Relationship skills

- Social awareness

- Cooperation

- Confidence

- Responsible decision-making

Game On

1. Have students form a circle.

2. Have the students all join hands.

3. Have two students in the circle let go of each other's hands. Place a hula hoop at the break, then have the two students rejoin hands through it.

4. Demonstrate how to maneuver through the hula hoop so that it passes over the entire body and on to the next person.

5. Have participants do this with the hula hoop, moving it around the entire circle until it reaches the starting point again.

6. Ask players to verbally encourage each person as he or she climbs through the hula hoop and sends it to the neighboring player without breaking the circle.

Add periodic quick-shares in the thick of game play, pausing the game to allow each student to share a one-word response to the last round of the game. These kinds of pauses can be used creatively by the leader to generate and harvest more Nurtured Heart acknowledgments: "Name one quality of greatness required for everyone to pass the hula hoop successfully." In this and other ways, intentionally nurture the hearts of the participants as the game progresses. Ask the group for creative ideas for new ways to pass the hula hoop or to change the game to add variety.

Look for Greatness

Energize:

- Cooperation and teamwork.

- Improvisation and creativity.

- Willingness to practice multiple times to gain mastery.

- Patience in waiting for a turn.

- Encouragement of other players.

- Compassion for different skill levels.

- Physical abilities like flexibility, mindfulness, dexterity, and control.

- Lending support and positivity to the group goal.

- Fostering friendship through extending all these great qualities to teammates.

Clarity for Players

No tugging or yanking on your neighbor's arm.

You must remain standing for the game.

No judgments or negative comments about anyone's attempts.

No arguing, roughhousing, bad words, or breaking any other of the general classroom rules while playing.

Let players know that you have faith they will be able to follow the rules of the game as well as the general group or classroom rules; and that, if necessary, you will reset them so they can get right back into the game.

Variations

Break the group into multiple circles and race to return the hula hoop to its original spot.

If only one group, use a timer in multiple trials to see if participants can improve their performance.

Add a second hula hoop to the circle, traveling in the opposite direction. Players now have to solve the problem of how to get the two hula hoops to cross through each other without releasing their hands. (Yes, it can be done!)

Ideas for Reflection

Encourage group members to give one or two recognitions to self and/or others participating about what they observed or appreciated. Create momentum for this by modeling as needed.

Start a conversation with the group about the experience of this game:

- "What were your favorite parts of the game and what greatness does that show?"

- "What surprised you about your fellow players?"

- "What strategies did you utilize or observe during the game?"

- "What was the biggest challenge?"

- "Did encouragement from others help?"

- "Was the game easier after you had more practice?"

- "Have you noticed that some things are easier for some people? What are some things that are easy for you to do? What are some things that are hard for you to do?"

If you added the more challenging variation of timing the group, ask them:

- "What was it like to be timed?"

- "Did you enjoy that challenge?"

- "How did you step up to the plate and make that challenge work for you?"

- "Are there other times that this is also necessary to do?"

Connect the lesson to life:

- "Can you think of some examples when encouraging others would be helpful? When you are participating in a race with a team, you encourage your teammate to keep going and pass the baton. When you're in class and someone is trying to formulate an answer, you can encourage them."

- "Is it more effective to pressure and rush others or encourage and support their effort?"

- "How does it affect you when your peers don't encourage you or get frustrated with your pace?"

- "Can you remember a time when others have encouraged you in the classroom or when you have encouraged others?"

Remind students of the qualities identified at the start of the lesson. Did they see what they predicted? Model by recognizing students with strong appreciation and acknowledgment. Examples: "I am really impressed by how cooperatively everyone worked on this challenge. You were fully engaged and supportive of your teammates. It really shows how present and thoughtful you were being during the game!" Support the conversation by asking what qualities they saw in others, in themselves, and in the group as a whole.

End the game and reflection time by acknowledging the group for its participation.

Walk Stop Wiggle Sit

Set Up

This game works well with any size group.

First, introduce the two basic movement patterns of Walk and Stop. "When I say walk, you walk, and when I say stop, you stop."

Have them do this for a brief few minutes. "Ready? Walk... Stop... Walk."

Let them know that the next step will be to do the *opposite* of what you say. When you say "walk," they will stop; and when you say "stop," they will walk. Also let them know that you will add more types of movement and stillness and that they should prepare to deeply listen, focus, and attend.

This game presents a great opportunity to talk about the skills of concentration, focus and listening and to actually practice them in the present moment.

This can be a great lesson in the observation of how our mind anticipates, which on one hand is great; however, thinking we know what's coming next will often inhibit the ability to listen.

SEL Skills

- Concentration and determination

- Handling frustration

- Emotional regulation

- Listening

Game On

1. Have students for a minute or so simply walk and stop, directly following your directions.

2. Then, switch it up. Tell students, "Now, do the opposite of what I say. When I say stop, walk; and when I say walk, stop."

3. Try this for a while. The students really have to focus and listen to respond correctly.

4. Then, introduce two additional commands: Wiggle and Sit. "When I say Wiggle, you wiggle, and when I say Sit, you sit." They will still be doing the opposite with Walk and Stop, but not with Wiggle and Sit. Very challenging!

5. Then, add in the reverse of Wiggle and Sit. "When I say wiggle, sit, and when I say sit, wiggle."

Look for Greatness

Energize:

- Great listening and attention to what is happening.
- Staying present for instructions while remaining on alert.
- Concentration in the face of anticipation.
- Willpower and perseverance to keep trying.
- Keen awareness of the physical boundaries of others and self.
- Enthusiasm and exuberance plus determination.
- Willingness to follow directions.
- A sense of humor.

THE GREATNESS OF BEING PRESENT AND FOCUSED

- Maintaining physical safety while accepting a challenge.

Clarity for Players

No intentional physical touching during the game.

No criticism of mistakes.

No arguing, roughhousing, bad words, or breaking any other of the general group rules while we are playing.

Let the players know that you have faith they will be able to follow the rules of the game as well as the general class rules; and that, if necessary, you will reset them so they can get right back into the game.

Variations

Play with other movement patterns and commands, such as fast and slow, left and right, or backward and forward.

Add in colors as commands; for example, "When I say green, that means go. Red means stop."

Have the kids brainstorm other commands.

Ideas for Reflection

Continue to build upon acknowledgments by encouraging group members to give one or two recognitions to self and/or others participating about what they observed or appreciated. Then add, "Is there anything you might do next time to notch it up?"

This game plays with the concepts of listening carefully, following directions, making mistakes and then resetting oneself:

- "What did you like about the game?"

- "Was it hard to stop your body, or to start wiggling, to walk or sit? Did you have fun even though those things were hard to do? What qualities does it take to have fun with something even though it is hard?"

- "What did it take to stop your bodies and do something else? Did you realize that you were resetting over and over and over again? Was it fun to reset and continue to play? What qualities does that take?"

Connect the lesson to life. Many times in life, when a shift is needed, one recognizes a need to make an adjustment:

- "Are there times at school where you make a mistake and you have to correct it, reset, and move on? When have you done that successfully before?"

- "What strategies have you used to reset yourself and move on from a mistake? In these instances, how do you reset yourself to the potential for greatness?"

- "Listening to instructions carefully is an important skill. Where are there times when it is important to listen carefully? Listening to your teacher give instructions for a test, listening to a doctor's advice, listening to your parents? Can you think of any others? What qualities of greatness are required for you to listen well? Awareness, patience, focus, attention, curiosity? What are some examples of your successes in doing that, today, or at other times?"

End the game and reflection time by acknowledging the group for its exceptional participation.

Acknowledgements and Resets
for Mindfulness Games

As you play these games, be sure to energize these qualities and any related character-building traits as they emerge, and to give participants many opportunities to see and energize them in each other. Acknowledgements with mindfulness games give the opening to help players bring awareness to what they are doing, just as the game itself is doing. When you speak about what you see in others, they get a reflection of what they are doing and the chance to self-appreciate and hone their focus.

Active Recognitions will register to the child as being seen and valued, and helps them observe themselves:

"You are moving both of your arms and you have your feet still on the ground. You are following the directions."

"You kept your gaze on your partner through the whole game."

"I noticed you started to answer that question and then paused for a few moments."

"You completely stopped your body when I said 'stop,' and you are still not moving."

"Becca, you were really sensitive in your appreciation of Rachel, using descriptive words to describe exactly why you are honoring her."

"Everyone is keeping their hands linked with their neighbors' hands without a single lapse."

Experiential Recognitions add expressive acknowledgement of qualities of character and greatness to Active Recognitions.

"Kim, you stopped playing when the game got too stressful. That takes great self-awareness and the ability to set boundaries for yourself."

"You made purposeful choices to keep your movements simple to begin with; I see you were allowing yourself to get into the momentum safely, and making it more fun by not overtaxing yourself. That takes incredible focus and determination, along with delight and ease about staying calm when no one else is."

"I noticed that every time we started moving again you moved your body in different ways. That takes creativity and motivation."

"I see your great qualities of discipline and intention because of the way you paid attention to my directions, and then kept to every single one – even while the game was chaotic."

"Marcus, your determination to not touch anyone showed radiantly. The result was visible in your attentiveness and actions. This reveals your beautiful integrity."

"Wow, that round only took us 25 seconds – five seconds less than the first time. All of us had the greatness of collaboration and teamwork."

Proactive Recognitions teach rules by energizing the child when the rules are being followed.

"Nancy, you were very resourceful in how you played this game. I saw the way you succeeded while following all the rules of respecting players' bodies, not shouting in other people's ears, and not bumping the furniture."

"I see you making positive choices with your body because you are making the choice to not touch the other players when you are moving."

"You really heard my rule for no yelling loudly. I see you regulating your voice all on your own. Whenever you started getting loud, you realized it, reset on your own and brought your voice back down. Thank you! You are modeling that rule for the rest of the class."

"Thank you for being in the game with persistence; even if you are tired, you are not breaking a single rule...you are remaining aware and in control of your actions!"

"The game was pretty crazy at times but you didn't let that craziness take over your body. Instead, you let yourself be crazy enough to have fun with everyone, but not so crazy that you didn't follow the rules. That shows beautiful control, purpose and clarity about where the line is."

"I noticed the three of you were standing too close for us to start the game, but before I could ask you to spread out, Nathan moved over, then Jacob, and you moved to another space too. Thank you, all! That reveals the greatness of your good judgment and initiative."

"That's really tricky, isn't it? Yet, you are not letting it frustrate you. Instead, you are laughing at how silly it is and having fun playing this game. I really appreciate how you are able to go with the flow and be playful even in a challenging situation. That takes self-confidence and maturity – both great qualities that I see in you."

Creative Recognitions lift up others by creating a simple, positive situation in which they cannot help but be successful.

"As I asked you to volunteer, Lisa, you were already raising your hand. I am in awe of your willingness and enthusiasm."

"I see your presence, Jeremy. Your eyes are completely focused, and this game calls for being focused to make it work."

"You two were just spacing yourselves appropriately for the game as we were moving to begin. You are helping the others to know what to do and keeping up the pace of the game. Thank you."

"You began the role I asked of you without complaining!"

"Jeremy, you came to the circle to join the game without asking questions. You are showing the greatness of trust and consideration."

"I was going to ask you to pick up that jacket so nobody stepped on it during the game, and you were already doing it. You knew what I was going to ask you to do before I could ask. You have the greatness of watchfulness and good judgment."

"Jack, thank you for using your voice so quietly to do what you needed to before rejoining the game. You didn't distract anyone in the process and now you're here. Welcome!"

Resets for Mindfulness Games

"Karen, the first time I said stop, you stopped your body and reset to the purpose in that moment, with a smile on your face. You have the greatness of resetting with joy and enthusiasm."

"Valerie, I saw you set boundaries with your fellow players with so much calmness and clarity. That was a kind way to reset everyone."

"Thank you for resetting to asking appropriate questions."

"Lindsay, you walked away from the game when it got to be too intense. I appreciate that you trusted yourself and knew you were better off taking a moment alone. That is brave and shows much wisdom!"

"Rachel, you reset your body to follow the rules of the game. Thank you."

"Class, you all reset yourselves, and are now looking at me to hear the next instruction. No one is talking. Thank you for your immense respect and attentiveness. I feel very honored as your teacher."

"Jimmy, reset... Jimmy, you got right back in your chair and reset your body to what we were doing. That requires responsibility and control over both your body and your emotions."

"Ron, you reset to trying really hard to articulate the qualities Lacy was showing during the game. You thought about giving up, but decided you were okay with being vulnerable, and then you freely showed how caring and attentive you are to your classmates.' Those are qualities of greatness I see in you. Thank you."

After giving Kyle a reset: "Kyle, you are now collaborating with Lisa to get the hula hoop over her head. You are doing this while being very attentive and patient, which shows great focus."

"You stopped wiggling your body and now you are sitting, just as I asked."

CHAPTER EIGHT

GREATNESS GAMES:

SEEING, EXPANDING, AND PLAYING WITH GREATNESS

These last games are about sharing, reflecting, and acknowledging greatness. They are wonderful inner wealth builders to follow any of the other games. They enhance awareness, help imprint learning, and encourage an overall experience of greatness and success for all participants. Reflection plays a crucial role in brain development and learning and in fostering empathy.

The overarching belief of the Nurtured Heart Approach is that everyone has inherent greatness and that we all flourish when those qualities of greatness are pointed out. Providing an admiring appreciation of such a quality and giving context for how that quality has showed up in that person tends to awaken them to owning those strengths for themselves. Children exposed to this style of sharing tend to accelerate their positive contributions and belief in their own positive attributes. Their compassion, wisdom, intuition, determination and other such qualities come to guide them and inspire others. They attain a growing sense of who they really are: people who possess greatness.

Because the games described are relatively simple and self-explanatory, this chapter uses a briefer version of the format used in earlier chapters.

♥ String of Beads

Set Up

This is a simple process of each player sharing a quality of greatness he or she sees in his/herself. A simple check-in process allows people to feel connected without going into a story. It is appropriate for groups of any size, seated in a circle.

You can choose to use a talking stick, passing it around so that when each person has the talking object, there is no cross talk. If the group is large, after an initial go at this activity in a large group, students can do this process in partners or smaller groups.

Game On

1. Get everyone seated comfortably, ready to listen to each other. Explain that this is a one-word check-in specifically meant to help them share a quality of greatness they see in themselves.

2. Go around the circle. Each participant names one great quality he or she observes in him/herself. Anyone can pass; check back in with to see if anyone who passed would like to share his or her one word before the game finishes.

Look for Greatness

Energize:

- Players sticking to the limit of only one word.

- Vulnerability in sharing genuine feelings.

- Courage in stretching to own new areas of greatness.

- Listening attentively to others' sharing in silence, without cross talk.

- Encouraging/supportive reactions to others' feelings.

Clarity for Players

No using more than one word unless specifically stated by facilitators that this is OK.

No cross talk or distracting behavior.

No disrespectful responses to others' sharing.

Variations

Share how you are feeling in terms of a weather report:

- "I'm feeling mostly sunny with a few clouds."

- "A bit stormy."

Other ways to share: a high and low of the day, a 'thorn' and a 'rose,' or something new in your life.

If the size of the group and time allow, try a second round where each participant gives a one- or two-word amplification to the quality he or she named in the first round. This helps inspire a spirit of excitement and play in turning up the dial on already-inspired greatness intentions. "Honesty" might become "passionate, consistent honesty" or "respect" might become "deep, committed, and openhearted respect."

 Greatness Circles

This is a simple, powerful way to support each other in seeing greatness.

Materials

You may wish to print out the qualities of greatness list included in this book so that all students have a reference to help them articulate what they are observing in others.

Set Up

This activity works best at the end of a group session, after participants have played other games.

Ask the group to form a seated circle.

Game On

1. Each person takes a turn speaking to the greatness they see exhibited in the group.

2. Have participants focus on specific, irrefutable truths.

Clarity for Players

No cross talk or distracting behavior.

No disrespectful responses to others' sharing.

Variations

Extend the game over the course of an entire school day: Pick a few qualities of greatness and put them up on the board at the beginning of the day or the group session. Have students keep an eye out during the day for times that this quality is expressed, and share it; or, they could post it on the board.

Give students the option to name a quality they are working on in themselves, and have one to three others in the circle give examples of how that person has expressed that quality during the games session or over the course of the school day.

The Web of Greatness and Appreciation

Materials

A ball of yarn.

Set Up

The group stands in a circle.

One person begins with a ball of yarn. She ties one loose end around her wrist, making a bracelet.

Game On

1. The first person tosses the ball of yarn to someone else, saying something she appreciates about that person's greatness.

2. That person then ties it around his wrist and tosses it to someone else, also giving an appreciation. Have the person standing next to the person who receives the ball help them tie the yarn or hold the ball – it's not easy to do both at once! – or let this happen spontaneously, and energize participants for being helpful.

3. On it goes until everyone has received the ball of yarn, creating an interconnected web.

4. After the web is complete, speak to how we are all interconnected; point out that we might as well be interconnected in greatness.

5. As everyone stands in the web of greatness, ask participants to share: How do their bodies feel? What emotions do they feel?

6. Cut the strings between players and trim off the excess. Everyone leaves the game with his or her own yarn greatness bracelet.

Look for Greatness

Energize:

- Original and authentic expressions of others' greatness.

- Offering or receiving assistance with tying the yarn bracelets.

- Attentive listening and expressions of caring.

- Remaining focused and remaining in the rhythm of the game.

- Responses given from a unique perspective.

- Stating greatness loud and clear.

Clarity for Players

No wildly throwing the ball of yarn.

No sarcastic appreciations.

No cross talk.

 Gratitude Ball

Materials

A soft foam ball.

Set Up

This game can be played in a circle, one participant at a time, or just popcorn-style in any seating arrangement.

Explain that this is the gratitude ball that is used by every group, collecting all that good energy.

Game On

1. Start tossing the ball from player to player.

2. As players catch the ball, they briefly share something they are grateful for in the moment, then toss the ball to another player.

3. After playing this version for a while, notch the game up by having participants give directed appreciations to the person receiving their toss, rather than having the catcher express gratitude.

Variations

Written appreciations: a great end-of-year activity. Each person folds paper into a card and puts his or her name on it. They pass their cards to the person to their left (or right) around the circle; each person writes an appreciation of that person on his or her card and continues to pass it along until it gets back to the person whose name is on it. Every student has a card full of appreciations to take home.

A fun variation on the ball toss is to use an imaginary ball. This works best in a circle, but can be done in any configuration as long as eye contact is made between the thrower and the catcher so that the catcher knows it is coming to him or her. The ball, as it takes in more goodness, expands a little with each toss. At the end it might be big enough to fill both arms of the last person to catch it. If you are in a circle configuration, the last person to catch the ball can be instructed to bring the ball to the center and have everyone help throw it up into the air, where it gently explodes, sending lots of good energy throughout the room, raining it down onto everyone present.

HOW TO BRING
NURTURED HEART PLAY
INTO EVERY ASPECT IN LIFE

There is an old Sanskrit word lila, which means play. Richer than our word, it means divine play. It also means love...
— Stephen Nachmanovich

As kids, we play spontaneously. Somewhere along the way, for most of us, getting into that mode requires more of an effort. We have to work to fit play into our busy schedules, and we rationalize it, saying we're doing it for the fitness and stress-reduction benefits.

Maybe adults could just re-learn to play for play's sake.

The play deficit is a real problem in today's world. Being entertained by a screen while sitting passively doesn't count as playing.

Fortunately, play and work are not opposites. We can bring lighthearted playfulness into all of our endeavors. Practice using the NHA is a wonderful support for a life lived playfully. Notice how the approach's techniques, including positive acknowledgements and resets – and even the refusal to energize negativity – can all be felt as a kind of play.

In all kinds of settings and for all ages, wherever people know how to point out the things their teammates are doing well and to notice their own successes, Nurtured Heart Play is transformative. This is true in professional business situations as well. Building each other up and making it fun is what it's all about. Developing new habit patterns of thought, speech, and action can be deep personal work that brings out the best in all your relationships, and it doesn't have to be heavy! Whatever the form of play, it can be enjoyed through the Nurtured Heart lens. Create games of greatness.

Throughout homes, schools, other organizations, clinics and therapists' offices that are using the Nurtured Heart Approach, children and adults are sharing successes with each other. They are acknowledging each other and the greatness qualities they exhibit each day. All over the world, ingenious educators, parents and therapists are creating greatness games to help them use the approach more effectively. One example: a teacher who picks a quality of greatness such as generosity or kindness out of a jar; and for the rest of the day or week, she looks for that quality in others, then shares it.

The three stands and the four recognitions create the structure for us all to be in a state of appreciation and to freely and sincerely share what is arising in our hearts. To speak with gratitude helps us all to learn how powerful empathy, compassion, consideration, cooperation and kindness are in supporting the growth of children and ourselves.

Building children's inner wealth helps them become the heroes of their own stories. Think about how to make this so for all children. Help them to realize their own greatness. Help them to see that hero within. Through your authentic appreciations of aspects of their greatness, expressed in gratitude, children come to a growing sense of who they really are: not the bad kid, or even the good kid, but the great kid, with great things to contribute.

In the Nurtured Heart Approach, there is an absolute belief that when children are made aware of their greatness, they live it. This takes an undeniable attitude of fearlessness. If you take the time to watch children playing fully, you'll see that they are often embracing their fearlessness: whether taking their first steps when learning to walk, being tossed in the air by a parent, climbing on the monkey bars, or running freely. Using the recognition techniques of NHA allows us to reflect to all children their incredible attributes of fearlessness, helping them to realize that this and the other incredible qualities they possess in play are also exhibited – and worth celebrating – in so many other areas of their lives. This will help them to see their own beauty and, ultimately, the beauty of others.

I hope these ideas add new dimensions of joy and connection to your life, bringing forth more positivity and greatness for everyone in your world!

RESOURCES

Here is a collection of resources for the Nurtured Heart Approach and more play and parenting resources to support you in lifelong learning:

💜 *Nurtured Heart Approach Books and Resources* ———

The Transforming the Intense Child Workbook: An Experiential Guide for Parents, Educators and Therapists for Learning and Implementing the Nurtured Heart Approach, by Howard Glasser with Melissa Lowenstein. Nurtured Heart Publications, 2016.

Transforming the Difficult Child, by Howard Glasser and Jennifer Easley. Nurtured Heart Publications, 1999 (Revised 2016)

Igniting Greatness, by Howard Glasser and Melissa Block. Nurtured Heart Publications, 2015.

Notching Up the Nurtured Heart Approach, by Howard Glasser and Melissa Lynn Block; Nurtured Heart Publications; 2011

ADHD Without Drugs: A Guide to the Natural Care of Children with ADHD, by Sanford Newmark, MD, with a foreword by Andrew Weil, MD. Nurtured Heart Publications, 2010.

All Children Flourishing: Igniting the Greatness of Our Children. Nurtured Heart Publications, 2008.

Books on Play, Education and Parenting

Parenting for Peace, by Marcy Axness, Ph.D. First Sentient Publications; 2012.

Playful Parenting, by Lawrence J. Cohen, Ph.D. Random House Publishing; 2001.

The Way of Mindful Education, by Daniel Rechtschaffen; W. W. Norton & Company; 2014

Whole Brain Child, by Dan J. Siegel, M.D. and Tina Payne Bryson, Ph.D.; Delacorte Press; 2011.

Play, by Stuart Brown, M.D., with Christopher Vaughn. Avery; 2009.

Spark, by John J. Ratey, M.D., with Eric Hagerman; Little Brown & Company. 2008

 Improv Books

Improv Wisdom, by Patrica Ryan Madson; Bell Tower of Random House; 2005

Playing Along, by Izzy Gessel; Whole Person Associates; 1997

Zoomy Zoomy, by Hannah Fox; Tusitala Publishing; 2010

 Play Organizations

Hand in Hand Parenting — Play-oriented resource for parents: www.handinhandparenting.org or (650) 322-5323

Great Activities Publishing Company — Great games for elementary educators. www.greatactivitiesonline.com or (800) 927-0682

Playworks — An organization helping to restructure recess in all major metropolitan areas. www.playworksinc.com or (864) 814-2230

Project Adventure — The premier experiential learning organization. Great resource for trainings and books on team building. www.project-adventure.org or (978) 542-4800

Life is Good Playmakers — Wonderfully affordable trainings for frontline caretakers of young children. www.lifeisgood.com or (503) 227-0803

Retribe — Great rites of passage programs for teens. www.retribe.org or (802) 371-5027

The Wayfinder Experience – A fantasy-role-playing theater camp for teens, based on the program originated by Howard Moody and Brian Allison. www.wayfinderexperience.com or (845) 481-0776

ACKNOWLEDGEMENTS

❤ Howard Moody

To Howard Glasser and Melissa Lowenstein, co-authors on this project: Thank you for making this happen. Thank you, Howard, for creating the Nurtured Heart Approach, and for the initial vision of this project. Everyone you meet feels your belief in the importance of connecting to one's heart and the power of expressing appreciation, joy, and creativity. Your continual support of the birthing of this book has been such a blessing in my life. Your seeing the greatness that I have within me and pushing me to bring it out in the writing of this book is deeply appreciated.

Melissa Lowenstein, your impeccable editing skills and deep understanding of play were invaluable to the completion of this book. You took my awkward meanderings and wove them together so beautifully, making this a book that I hope will be a support to many people.

Special thanks to Valerie Potts, whose friendship, support, and availability for *many* phone conversations have been a true gift throughout this whole project. You truly embody the Nurtured Heart Approach, and without you, I could not have written this book.

A shout-out to Sarah How, Vivian Barajas, Stephanie Rule, and Lyla Tyler, all of whom contributed stories for this book. You took the play concepts and games we sent you and used your creativity and genius to test them and weave in aspects of the NHA. Your work provided validation we needed to actualize what we felt was true: that play and the Nurtured Heart Approach were a natural fit. Thank you!

To my best friend, Brian Allison: your friendship and support made it possible for me to complete this project. To all of my friends at Omega Institute: I felt your continual support as I huddled in the corner of the café, typing away.

Thank you to everyone I have met in the Nurtured Heart community. Your passion and commitment to the greatness in all children is inspiring. Special thanks to Ivri Turner for arranging for me to share play with the participants at the first Certification Training Intensive (CTI) I attended.

Thank you to all the parents, teachers, counselors, therapists, health professionals, and school administrators who are committed to the health, happiness and well-being of children. May you find this book helpful in your journey.

And finally: to all the children and teens with whom I have had the opportunity to play. Your spirit, playfulness, imagination and joy are a true gift to us all.

Melissa Lowenstein

Thanks to Howard Moody for creating this skillful inter-weaving of play and nurturing hearts. I'm a big believer in play as the best teacher. I know I learn best when I'm having fun! Howard M., your perseverance and dedication in this project were inspiring to me.

Thanks to Howard Glasser for holding everyone's feet to the proverbial fire (of greatness), insisting that we push these games into next levels of fidelity with the NHA. I believe the hard work was totally worth it. Howard G., you always hold the higher vision in every project, and you never bow to my mildly pathologic tendency to barrel headlong toward completion rather than taking the time to fit all the pieces together with integrity and clarity.

Thanks to Alice Glasser for her great insights and supportive ideas, particularly around how to organize and flesh out the descriptions of individual games.

And thanks to all those dedicated NHA warriors out there who are bringing transformation where it can make the biggest difference: in the lives of children and families and on the campuses of schools.

Howard Glasser

I hold great admiration and gratitude for those who brought this project to fruition through many junctures of questioning and reconfiguring. Thank you so much, Howard Moody, for your beautiful vision, dedication, and purpose – and, most of all, your perseverance. There were so many points at which you could have thrown your hands up in frustration, and I am so appreciative of you not only hanging in there but for doing so with the most amazingly kind attitude. Here's to a vision of your great impact on the new world of play and its brimming possibilities as a vehicle for children learning about their greatness.

Melissa Lowenstein: Once again you have dug in deep, shining your brilliance in rewrite after rewrite, re-conception after re-conception, finding a way through, languaging the merger between the world of play and the world of the Nurtured Heart Approach. No one on the planet better could have done it better than you.

Alice Glasser: Thank you so much for your dedication to Howard's dream of conveying his wisdom and unfolding it in the gift and beauty of your artwork. Thank you for serving on this project as cover artist and art director and in your brilliant rewrite and consolidation of the ultimate format design that made this the great contribution to NHA we had hoped for. You came through over and over, and I am so grateful.

Thank you so much to Kay Paden for such valuable feedback about format and game design in making this work optimally accessible to educators – especially your nudge to incorporate a lens of Social Emotional Learning.

Thank you to all those who did trial runs of these games to test how transposable these skills were, and how they intermeshed with the Nurtured Heart Approach in practice. My great appreciation to Valerie Potts, Lyla Tyler, and Viviana Barajas for your amazing feedback and personal stories.

Once again, a great thank you to Owen DeLeon. Your amazing graphic arts talents are only exceeded by your dedication and patience. It is such a pleasure to work with you and to have you so incredibly able to take every ounce of our feedback into next steps in making this book great. You are at the heart of this inspired team effort. Thank you.

And lastly, my deep gratitude to our friends at the Children Success Foundation and to all the Nurtured Heart Approach trainers worldwide.

Howard Glasser, 2017 – Tucson, Arizona

ABOUT THE AUTHORS

💜 Howard Moody

Howard Moody has been facilitating play in many forms for over 25 years. He specializes in designing team building, stress reduction, and wellness presentations that are full of play, joy and laughter.

Howard has been also been a teacher and successful coach of numerous sports for many years and deeply understands the value of creating effective teams and how to achieve peak performance.

His initial interest in play started as an athlete but turned more toward alternative recreation when he took training's with the New Games foundation, Project Adventure, and in Original Play and improvisational theater.

Howard has been (and is still currently) a core faculty member at the Omega Institute for Holistic Studies for many years and he is also the co-founder of The Adventure Game Theater, an extraordinary improvisational learning process for teens that has been featured in *Mothering* magazine and on PBS and NPR. Combining experiential learning with creativity, improvisational theater, play, community building, mythology and storytelling the Adventure Game Theater has brought magic into many young people's lives. He is currently on the faculty of Retribe, a dynamic rites of passage program for teens that incorporates Adventure Game theater into its transformational programming.

Deepening connections among people is Howard's passion and his mission is to help people be fully inspired, creative and playful in all that they do. Howard is a certified Advanced Trainer for the Nurtured Heart Approach.

Howard can be reached at www.howardmoody.com or 845-679-2043.

Howard Glasser

Howard Glasser is the Founder and Board Chairman of the Children's Success Foundation and creator of the Nurtured Heart Approach.

He is dedicated to awakening the greatness in all children, with a particular focus on intense and challenging children.

Howard is the author of *Transforming the Difficult Child*, currently the top-selling book on difficult children, as well as several other books designed to unfold the Nurtured Heart Approach for educators, therapists, and parents.

Howard has been called one of the most influential living persons working to reduce children's reliance on psychiatric medications.

He has been a featured guest on CNN, a consultant for 48 Hours, and featured in *Esquire* Magazine.

His work is currently being researched at the University of Arizona and Rutgers University.

Alice Glasser ——

Alice Glasser is an artist and graphic designer, and a certified Nurtured Heart Approach Advanced Trainer. She helps her father on various creative projects, editing and visually interpreting. She is currently living and working in New Zealand, supporting her church.

Melissa Lowenstein (formerly Block) ———

Melissa is a writer and editor who has co-authored multiple books on the Nurtured Heart Approach with Howard Glasser. She is a certified NHA trainer (since 2008), a youth program facilitator, yoga teacher, and parent and step-parent to a total of five amazing children ranging in age from 12 to 23.

—